The Bes

Pressure Cooker

Cookbook Ever

The Best
Pressure Cooker
Cookbook Ever

Pat Dailey

A John Boswell Associates/King Hill Productions Book

HarperCollins*Publishers*

HarperCollins books may be purchased for educational, business, or sales promotional use. For information, please write: Special Markets Department, HarperCollins Publishers, Inc., 10 East 53rd Street, New York, NY 10022.

Design: Barbara Cohen Aronica
Index: Maro Riofrancos

Library of Congress Cataloging-in-Publication Data

Dailey, Pat.
    The best pressure cooker cookbook ever / Pat Dailey.—1st ed.
        p.   cm.
    Includes index.
    ISBN 0-06-017092-1
    1. Pressure cookery.   I. Title.
TX840.P7D34   1994
641.5'87—dc20   94-12070

94 95 96 97 98 HC 10 9 8 7 6 5 4 3

Contents

STEWS AND ONE-DISH MEALS 66

The pressure cooker really stars when it speeds up normally long-simmering dishes, such as Chicken and Sausage Gumbo, Beef Carbonnade with Caramelized Onions, Pork, Potato, and Sauerkraut Goulash, and Moroccan Lamb and Eggplant Stew.

PASTA AND PASTA SAUCES 96

Whether sauced separately or cooked together in the pressure cooker in 3 minutes flat, pasta is a breeze with recipes such as Spicy Marinara Sauce, Bolognese Ragu, Ravioli with Gorgonzola and Sage Cream, and Tortellini with Prosciutto and Peas.

BEANS AND LENTILS 107

Now dried beans can be a last-minute thought or part of a quick supper. Smokin' Red Beans and Rice, Ponderosa Pintos, Almost No-Fat Refried Beans, and Lentil Slaw are a few of the tasty choices.

RICE AND GRAINS 124

Effortless Wheat Berry Tabbouleh, Wild Mushroom Risotto, and Barley and Vegetable Pilaf are among the types of recipes the pressure cooker does perfectly.

VEGETABLES 142

With a delicate touch even under pressure, you'll turn out a brilliant variety of vegetable dishes: Creamy Braised Potatoes and Leeks with Bacon, Broccoli with Parmesan Cheese, Provençal Artichoke Ragout, and Summer Green Beans with Tomato and Pesto.

DESSERTS   **170**

*Chocolate Caramel Custard, Brown Sugar Bread Pudding, Classic
Cheesecake, and Wine-Mulled Peaches are among the types of sweets the
pressure cooker does best.*

INDEX   **190**

Introduction

Using Your Pressure Cooker to Beat the Clock

Kitchens today are filled with many questions: How can meals be made more quickly? Is it possible to have an element of control over nutrition? Is there a way to save money, but not at the sacrifice of time? When will dinner be ready? Harried cooks are left to scramble for solutions that range from frozen foods to phone orders. Too many overlook one of the best solutions—the pressure cooker. This overlooked ally is in fact the answer to many of the questions and conflicts that rear up at meal time. A sleek pot with a lock, a valve, and a gentle hiss, the pressure cooker embraces the creative urge to cook stylishly and with sound nutrition; yet it doesn't stifle with unrealistic demands on time or skills.

Pressure cookers are quick (sometimes extraordinarily so), versatile, and well suited to a full menu of contemporary tastes. A pressure cooker can turn out a pot of gumbo in ten minutes, steamed broccoli in five. Rice is a ten-minute exercise, and dried beans take little longer than that. The comfort of a hearty stew can grace the table in half an hour; the finesse of a classic fish soup comes more quickly than a carry-out pizza. Marvelously flavored soups, simmering stews, and hearty one-dish meals with strength and character are among the expected accomplishments of the pressure cooker. Quick pasta dishes, delicate fish entrees, and devilishly decadent desserts are the serendipitous surprises it also offers.

If the pressure cooker is not a basic tool in everyone's battery of kitchen equipment, it may be because many family histories include at least one explosive saga of such a pot gone awry. In an earlier generation, pressure cookers didn't have the elaborate safety systems with double-default backups that endow their modern counterparts. Spaghetti sauce accidentally painted walls tomato red, projectile lamb shanks dented ceilings, and beef stew became an unwelcome garment instead of dinner, or so the stories say. The chief drawback in the early designs was that they allowed for human error. Almost all mishaps took place when the cover was removed before pressure had been fully dissipated. Modern designs make that impossible, so that pressure cooking now is assuredly safe and pleasurable.

Early editions of *The Joy of Cooking,* the unfailingly trusted culinary adviser of several generations of cooks, recognized the enormous appeal of pressure cookers. Referring to them in the 1940s, author Irma S. Rombauer wrote, "There is a gadget on the market that permits a cook to scoff at time." So go ahead, scoff at the clocks at mealtime, and let the pressure cooker take the pressure off you.

The Pressure Principle

Most cooks are not hungry for scientific discourses on physics, chemistry, and complex molecular reactions that explain why foods cook the way they do. Rather, just serving up the tasty evidence is proof enough that some wonderful sort of culinary alchemy has taken place. Red meat turns brown and luscious. Rice turns from rock-hard to fluffy and tender. Carrots transform into a smooth puree. But pressure cooking is so unique, so unlike most other cooking methods, a brief explanation of how it works is in order.

Everyday slang offers clues to the pressure principle. Things are said to heat up when the pressure is on. Precisely the same thing happens inside a pressure cooker. Take a close look at your pressure cooker. Then read on for a few insights into this seemingly magical method of cooking.

Imagine the pressure cooker sitting on the stove, uncovered and filled with boiling water. The water bubbles away and a cloud of steam hovers above the pan. Now think of the same cooker and the same boiling water, but with a cover on. Not just any lid, but the slightly modified one that distinguishes a pressure cooker from all the other pots. Tucked inside the rim of a pressure cooker's lid is a rubber sealing gasket that makes the pressure cooker absolutely airtight. This simple addition means that once inside the pressure cooker, nothing gets out, including the cloud of steam created by boiling water.

Because it can't escape, the steam generated by the heat builds up pressure inside the cooker. First 5 pounds, then 10 pounds, and soon after, 15 pounds of pressure have generated, and you have a pressure cooker going at full speed. Simple enough. Now consider another basic scientific fact. The increased pressure bears down on the surface of the liquid in the cooker, filling up all the space between the top of the food and the inside of the cover. Given their druthers, the heated water molecules in the cooking liquid would break up to create even more steam. But since there is nowhere for them to go in the closed pot, they're inhibited and restrained. They get a little bit antsy then and move around faster, thus creating more friction and heat in the food.

At sea level, the boiling point is 212 degrees. Add 15 pounds of pressure—the maximum amount attainable in a pressure cooker—and the boiling point increases to 250 degrees. Going back to the same pot of boiling water, its temperature in an uncovered pot is 212 degrees, but in a covered pressure cooker it can reach 250 degrees. This increased temperature is primarily what makes foods cook so much faster in a pressure cooker.

Buried in the above explanation is an important principle of pressure cooking. You need liquid to create the steam that builds the pressure. This is why soups cook so well in the pressure cooker and brownies don't. Or why you can't bake a lamb chop or roast a turkey; there's not enough liquid. If you put food in a pressure cooker without enough liquid, it will burn in fairly short order.

Besides generating a lot of heat, the pressure cooker helps things along in another way. The increased pressure goes to work on tough, fibrous parts of food, easing them apart and making them fork-tender. (And meanwhile, all the flavors are sealed inside the pot.) So, you see, it's not magic, and it's not mysterious microwaves that speed things up in the pressure cooker: It's the safe principles of Science 101.

Safety

Now back to those blown lids and fearsome reputations of yesteryear. With nary a single incident where I felt the cleanliness of my kitchen ceiling or the sanctity of my personal safety were in jeopardy, it's easy to drift toward flippancy. Older model pressure cookers do allow for accidents. Fortunately, in what are being called the "new generation" of pressure cookers, it's virtually impossible for such missteps to take place. A pressure release valve at the top of the pot prevents more than 15 pounds of pressure from building inside the pot. If you forget to adjust the heat downward once full pressure is attained, the cooker will let off a persistent hiss that releases the extra steam. Additionally, a locking mechanism on the handle is designed so the pot cannot be opened until the pressure inside has returned to normal.

Most manufacturers of cookers sold in the United States voluntarily submit their units to Underwriters Laboratories. There, a team of crafty technicians doggedly and deviously do everything to pressure cookers that you're not supposed to do: override safety valves, build up too much pressure, and generally abuse them—all in the name of safety. This satisfies the folks at UL that there is no possibility that normal use plus a margin of error could cause a mishap. Once they're convinced, they award it with approval, more than enough to convince me that the model is 100 percent safe.

If you have an old pressure cooker and are comfortable using it, then please continue, always remembering to use caution and follow the instructions.

However, I don't recommend that new users begin with an inherited model from an aunt, grandmother, or garage sale. A new model is a better bet.

A few commonsense principles apply, however, even to new cookers. *Do not deep-fry* foods in a covered pressure cooker. Do not ever try to force the cooker or tamper with the valve. Follow the maintenance advice in your owner's manual about cleaning the valve. A final safety note comes as a cautionary warning. The food inside a pressure cooker is much hotter than other foods you've cooked. Be sure to let them cool sufficiently before dipping in your tasting spoon.

Makes and Models

There are two basic designs in pressure cookers, both of which were used in testing recipes for this book. The first borrows liberally from early models and features a removable pressure regulating weight that sits atop the cooker. It dances around a bit, ever so quietly chugging away as a gentle reminder that it's in use. As a matter of course, these models also tend to let off a little bit of steam as they cook (hence, they sometimes will require more liquid to cook foods properly). These do not measure the pounds of pressure inside the pot. There are a handful of recipes in the book—mostly chicken—that I felt cooked a little better with 5 pounds of pressure instead of a full 15 pounds. However, these can be made in cookers with no pressure setting; alternative timing is included.

The second design is full of modern enhancements, and these models usually show off with sleek designs as well. Needless to say, they carry a higher price tag, too, although there is a range of prices in this category, and most budgets should be able to accommodate one if it suits your cooking style. In these, the pressure regulator is built into the cover and features a calibrated rod that peeks up as more pressure builds up inside. They also feature heavier, stainless steel construction, and they sometimes have a "sandwich" of metals in the bottom to conduct heat better.

A range of sizes of pressure cookers is available, from two-quart to ten-quart or more, with six-quart cookers the most common. As you consider which type is best suited to your needs, keep in mind that a pressure cooker can only be filled about two-thirds of the way. This means a six-quart cooker holds a maximum of four quarts of combined solids and liquid. Most models indicate the maximum fill line. Adhere to this except when cooking beans and rice, when cookers should only be filled halfway. Of course, they don't have to be filled to capacity. Lesser amounts of food can be prepared. Also, the pressure cooker can be used for conventional cooking. Either uncovered or covered but unlocked, it acts just like any other heavy saucepan.

Almost every model comes with a trivet or cooking rack, which raises foods off the bottom of the cooker. Many also come with a removable steamer insert. A steamer insert is invaluable for simple steaming of vegetables. If your cooker does not include one, check to see if it can be ordered from the manufacturer.

One of the most important accessories that comes with every pressure cooker is the instruction book. I hope you'll resist the typical trend of merely glancing at your pressure cooker's instruction book to figure out how to get the cover off. It deserves to be read, cover to cover. (I know, you really don't want to: but try it anyway.) The manufacturer knows best how their model works. What they say goes. Makes and models vary, and from the instruction book you'll gain valuable insights and tips about using your particular cooker. You'll learn how much liquid they suggest using, how and when to clean the valve, and if the cooker is dishwasher safe.

Getting Started

In case you've skipped everything else up to this point, this is the real nitty-gritty you need to know before jumping into the recipes. For most accurate timing, place a cooker over high heat until the desired pressure is reached. Then, adjust it down to maintain the proper pressure. Pressure cookers are very efficient, and in most cases, the lowest heat setting will be sufficient to maintain pressure.

When cooking is completed, there are several ways to release pressure in a pressure cooker:

1. For natural pressure release: After the allotted cooking time, simply turn off the heat and let the cooker sit until the indicator shows that all pressure has been released. In this method, foods continue to cook from residual heat, so it isn't suggested for delicate foods where overcooking will detract from them. Most soups and stews are fine candidates for natural pressure release. An advantage for many foods is that left covered and locked, the food will stay hot for several hours.

2. For quick release: A method that applies to all cookers is to carry the cooker to the sink and run cold water over the cover. Within seconds, the pressure falls to normal. I suggest this method routinely throughout the book. Just be sure to use a heavy mitt and clear the sink before you start.

Many models also have a steam release mechanism on the handle, which allows you to open a valve and quickly release the pressure-building steam. Though this has advantages, it does emit a lot of steam in the process. Be sure to turn the steam vent away from you as pressure is released.

In each recipe, estimated cooking times are given. Unless otherwise indicated, the timing begins once high pressure is reached. Depending on a number of factors, such as the amount and density of the food and the amount of liquid, it can take from 1 to 10 minutes or longer to reach high pressure. Several recipe categories are timed a little differently. Timing for many vegetable and fish recipes begins as soon as the pressure cooker is placed over high heat. This is clearly noted in the recipes. All recipes in this book were tested in a six-quart cooker, although most can also be made in a four-quart model with no adjustments.

Carry one more thought into the kitchen with you as you begin with a pressure cooker. All cooking methods take a little getting used to. Trial and error are part of a learning curve that fortunately comes pretty quickly. I hope each and every recipe in this book will reward you with unrivaled success. But if a glitch arrives in the form of overcooked carrots or a less than masterful stew, don't worry. As with crêpes and pancakes, subsequent batches will be much better. Now, jump in and enjoy your pressure cooker.

Soups and Stocks

Edna Ferber once wrote that "Roast beef, medium, is not only a food. It is a philosophy." So considered, soup rises to Aristotelian heights. While I certainly could mutter a few choice comments about a slice of beef, I could rhapsodize endlessly on the merits and meaning of soup. Soup is substance and comfort; it is quiet, unassuming pleasure and tantalizing aroma. Most importantly, it is exactly what the cook wants it to be. Chilled soups relieve the scorch of summer, while the robust recipes of winter warm and smooth over harsh edges. Myriad forms, from light broths to creamy chowders, fit almost any occasion.

Pressure cookers surely provide one of the easiest, quickest, and most foolproof ways to prepare soup. Cooks who are just becoming acquainted with their pressure cooker will do well to begin the journey by making soup. The soup pot always is forgiving, and it makes accommodations for less than perfect form. It also allows the cook a lot of leeway in changing ingredients around. To wit, a friend made the Italian lentil soup with sausage and peppers, noting that she decreased the amount of sausage, added some wine, and used kale. Her changes came about as she peered into cupboards and the refrigerator and saw what was on hand. The soup worked just as well, yet it was different, and in its own way, uniquely hers.

I've included many different styles of soup, from pleasing summer chillers to silken purees and "big bowl" concoctions filled with chunky meats and vegetables. Besides offering their own unique pleasures, these recipes can be used as guides to help you make your own favorite soups in the pressure cooker. Here are a few things to keep in mind:

- Make sure ingredients don't go beyond the maximum capacity of your cooker.
- When adapting your own nonpressure cooker soup recipes, decrease the amount of liquid slightly to compensate for the lack of evaporation.
- If a recipe includes grains or meats, which take a long time to cook, cook the soup in two stages, adding the vegetables toward the end of the cooking so their texture and character remain intact.
- Most soups, like stews, have the welcome habit of improving after a day or two. Make extras and double the pleasure when you reheat them.

Fresh Tomato Basil Soup

Summer rarely comes to the table more clearly than when perfect, sun-ripened tomatoes are part of the menu. Here they are transformed into a rosy soup that is the essence of summer. Serve the soup with a swirl of fresh pesto or accompanied by thin slices of toasted Italian bread spread with goat cheese.

Makes 4 servings

---

2 tablespoons olive oil
1 garlic clove, minced
1 small onion, minced
2½ to 3 pounds vine-ripened tomatoes,
   cored, seeded, and coarsely chopped

3 tablespoons chopped fresh basil
1 to 2 teaspoons balsamic vinegar
Salt and freshly ground pepper

---

1. Heat 1 tablespoon oil in the pressure cooker. Add the garlic and onion and cook uncovered over medium heat until they begin to soften, 3 to 4 minutes. Add tomatoes.

2. Cover and bring up to high pressure. Reduce heat to stabilize pressure and cook 8 minutes. Release pressure.

3. Strain the solids from the liquid, reserving both. Puree the tomato solids and basil in a food processor or blender. Add reserved liquid to thin to serving consistency. Stir in the remaining oil and vinegar. Season with salt and pepper to taste. Serve hot or chilled.

Avocado Bisque

The addition of aromatic vegetables to a classic avocado soup results in a refined finish. A sprinkle of fresh herbs at serving time can tailor the soup to many menus. Cilantro plays to its Tex-Mex side, while fresh mint accentuates its Middle Eastern tones.

Makes 3 to 4 servings

---

1 tablespoon unsalted butter
2 small celery ribs, chopped
1 small onion, chopped
I small zucchini, chopped
1 jalapeño pepper, seeded if desired, minced
2 cups Chicken Stock (page 25) or Vegetable Stock (page 24)

½ teaspoon ground cumin
½ teaspoon dried mint
2 large ripe avocados, peeled and pitted
⅓ cup whipping cream
Salt

---

1. Melt butter in the pressure cooker over medium heat. Add the celery, onion, zucchini, and jalapeño. Cook uncovered until vegetables begin to soften, 3 to 4 minutes. Add stock, cumin, and mint.

2. Cover and bring up to high pressure. Reduce heat to stabilize pressure and cook 5 minutes. Release pressure.

3. Puree the contents of the cooker in a blender or food processor. Add the avocados and blend again until smooth. Transfer to a serving container and stir in cream and salt to taste. Serve hot or chilled.

Basque Potato and Sausage Soup

Rustic ingredients make a hearty winter meal. Red cabbage slaw and whole wheat bread are fine meal partners for the soup.

Makes 3 to 4 servings

8 ounces smoked hot sausage, sliced ½ inch thick

1 medium onion, cut in ¾-inch chunks

2 small celery ribs, bias-cut ¾ inch thick

2 medium tomatoes, cut into 1-inch chunks

1 large red potato, unpeeled, cut into ½-inch dice

1½ cups Chicken Stock (page 25) or canned broth

1 teaspoon dried thyme

Salt and freshly ground pepper

1. Combine the sausage and onion in the pressure cooker. Cook uncovered over medium-high heat, stirring often, until the sausage is browned, 4 to 5 minutes. Add the celery, tomatoes, potato, chicken broth, and thyme.

2. Cover and bring up to high pressure. Reduce heat to stabilize pressure and cook 8 minutes. Release pressure and season with salt and pepper to taste.

Tortilla Vegetable Soup

Through ages and cultures, cooks have found clever uses for leftovers. In this case, day-old corn tortillas thicken soup broth and imbue it with their distinct flavor. Only vegetables are used here, although leftover bits of cooked chicken or turkey can be added.

Makes 4 servings

---

3 corn tortillas, torn into pieces

1½ cups Chicken Stock (page 25) or canned broth

2 medium carrots, bias-cut into 1½-inch pieces

2 celery ribs, bias-cut into 1½-inch pieces

2 ears of sweet corn, husked and cut or broken into 4 pieces

½ small head green cabbage, cut into 4 pieces

1 can (8 ounces) tomato sauce

1 teaspoon chili powder

1 scallion

1 jalapeño or serrano pepper

⅓ cup cilantro leaves

4 lime wedges

---

1. Combine the tortillas and stock or broth in the pressure cooker. Cover the pressure cooker and bring up to high pressure. Immediately remove from heat and release pressure. Carefully transfer contents to a blender or food processor and puree.

2. Return tortilla puree to the pressure cooker and add carrots, celery, corn, cabbage, tomato sauce, and chili powder. Cover and bring up to high pressure. Reduce heat to stabilize pressure and cook 4 minutes. Release pressure.

3. Mince the scallion, jalapeño pepper, and cilantro together. Sprinkle some over each bowl of soup and serve each with a lime wedge.

Thai-Flavored Eggplant Soup

Coconut milk enriches this silky potage and also cools the heat of the curry. Thai curry pastes are available in the Asian food sections of many supermarkets.

Makes 4 to 6 servings

---

1 tablespoon olive oil
1 small onion, minced
2 teaspoons fresh ginger, minced
2 slender eggplants, preferably Italian, peeled and cubed
1 medium red potato, peeled and sliced
2 cups Chicken Stock (page 25) or canned broth

½ to 1 teaspoon Thai red or green curry paste
¼ cup cilantro leaves
¼ cup fresh basil leaves
¼ cup coconut milk
Salt

---

1. Heat oil in the pressure cooker. Add the onion and ginger. Cook uncovered over medium heat until soft and fragrant, 4 to 5 minutes. Add the eggplant, potato, stock or broth, and curry paste. Cover and bring up to high pressure. Reduce heat to stabilize pressure and cook 8 minutes. Release pressure.
2. Strain the solids from the liquid, reserving both. Transfer the solids to a food processor or blender and add cilantro and basil. Puree until smooth. Stir in the reserved cooking liquid and coconut milk. Season with salt to taste. Serve hot.

Cauliflower Cheese Soup with Red Chile

Pure ground red chile adds an earthy edge to a creamy cauliflower soup.

Makes 4 to 6 servings

---

1 tablespoon unsalted butter
1 medium onion, chopped
1 teaspoon pure ground red chile
½ teaspoon ground cumin
1 medium head of cauliflower, about
   1½ pounds, sliced
1 medium red potato, peeled and
   sliced

2¼ cups Chicken Stock (page 25) or
   Vegetable Stock (page 24)
1½ cups (6 ounces) shredded mild
   cheese such as Chihuahua, brick, or
   Muenster
¾ cup half-and-half or whole milk
Salt and freshly ground pepper
⅔ cup tomato salsa

---

1. Melt butter in the pressure cooker. Add the onion, chile, and cumin. Cook uncovered over medium heat until the onion begins to soften, about 3 minutes. Add the cauliflower, potato, and stock.

2. Cover and bring up to high pressure. Reduce heat to stabilize pressure and cook 6 minutes. Release pressure.

3. Puree soup in batches in a blender or food processor. Return to the pressure cooker; add cheese and half-and-half or milk. Cook over low heat until cheese is melted, 2 minutes. Season with salt and pepper to taste. Remove from heat. Swirl a large spoonful of salsa into each serving.

Tuscan Pasta, Potato, and Bean Soup

Tuscans are called mangiafagiole, *"bean eaters," by other Italians—a reference to their predilection for beans. They have many wonderful ways of preparing them, including this rich, rib-sticking soup.*

Makes 6 servings

½ cup white or navy beans, soaked
    overnight
3 tablespoons olive oil
2 small celery ribs, diced
1 small carrot, diced
1 large garlic clove, minced
Pinch of crushed hot pepper flakes
2 medium red or white potatoes,
    peeled and sliced

2 cups water
¼ cup fresh basil
2 small tomatoes, seeded and finely
    diced
1 small roasted red pepper, finely diced
1 cup dried multicolored wagon wheel
    pasta, cooked according to package
    directions
Salt and freshly ground pepper

---

1. Heat half of the oil in the pressure cooker. Add celery, carrot, garlic, and hot pepper flakes. Cook uncovered over medium heat until the vegetables are tender, about 5 minutes. Add beans, potatoes, and water.

2. Cover and bring up to high pressure. Reduce heat and cook 10 minutes. Release pressure.

3. Carefully transfer the contents of the cooker to a food processor or blender. Add basil and puree until smooth. Add additional water if needed to thin the soup. Return puree to cooker and stir in the tomatoes, diced red pepper, pasta, salt and pepper, and rest of the oil. Cook gently to heat through.

Santa Fe Sweet Potato Chowder with Chorizo

Makes 4 to 6 servings

4 ounces chorizo sausage, removed
   from casing
1 medium onion, chopped
1 jalapeño or serrano pepper, seeded
   and minced
1 pound sweet potatoes, peeled and
   sliced
½ teaspoon ground cumin

2½ to 3 cups Chicken Stock
   (page 25) or canned broth
1 can (16 ounces) hominy, drained
1 cup sweet corn kernels (fresh or
   thawed frozen)
1 medium tomato, diced
½ cup half-and-half or light cream
¼ cup chopped fresh cilantro
Salt and freshly ground pepper

1. Crumble chorizo in the pressure cooker and cook uncovered over medium-high heat until browned, 3 to 5 minutes. Remove chorizo with a slotted spoon and drain on paper towels.

2. Add the onion and jalapeño pepper to cooker. Cook, stirring often, until the onion begins to soften, about 3 minutes. Add the sweet potatoes, cumin, and 2½ cups stock or broth.

3. Cover and bring up to high pressure. Reduce heat to stabilize pressure and cook 7 minutes. Release pressure.

4. Carefully transfer the contents of the cooker to a blender or food processor. Puree until smooth. Return to cooker and add chorizo and hominy, corn kernels, tomato, half-and-half, cilantro, and salt and pepper to taste; heat gently. Add additional ½ cup stock if soup is too thick.

Boniato Soup

The boniato is a gnarly tuber commonly used in island cuisines. Its bland taste and starchy texture are used to fine advantage in a soup that is spicy and rich. Boniatos can be found in many large urban markets and smaller Latin or Caribbean groceries. Use potatoes if you can't find them.

Makes 4 to 6 servings

1 tablespoon unsalted butter
1 medium onion, minced
1 small garlic clove, minced
¼ teaspoon ground cumin
1½ pounds boniato, peeled and sliced
3½ to 4 cups Chicken Stock
    (page 25) or canned broth

1 small piece of fresh ginger, about ½
    inch square, peeled
1 jalapeño or serrano pepper, seeded if
    desired
⅓ cup whipping cream
Salt and cayenne
Chopped fresh cilantro, for garnish

1. Melt the butter in the pressure cooker over medium heat. Add the onion, garlic, and cumin. Cook uncovered over medium heat, stirring, until soft, about 5 minutes. Add boniato and 3½ cups chicken stock or broth.

2. Cover and bring up to high pressure. Reduce heat to stabilize pressure and cook 5 minutes. Release pressure.

3. Strain the solids from the liquid, reserving both. Puree solids along with ginger and jalapeño pepper in a food processor or blender. Stir the puree back into the cooking liquid. Add cream, salt, and cayenne. Add additional ½ cup stock if soup is too thick. Garnish with a sprinkling of cilantro.

Bayou Black-Eye Pea Bisque

Black-eye peas cook quick as a wink in the pressure cooker. Here, they're prepared as a soup that mimics the classic Southern bean dish hoppin' John.

Makes 6 to 8 servings

1½ cups dried black-eye peas, soaked
   overnight
3 tablespoons olive oil
3 celery ribs, sliced
1 medium onion, chopped
2 jalapeño or serrano peppers, seeded
   and minced
2 large garlic cloves, minced
¾ cup diced smoked ham (3 ounces)

4 cups Chicken Stock (page 25) or
   Vegetable Stock (page 24)
1½ teaspoons Creole spice blend
¼ cup chopped fresh cilantro
½ cup half-and-half
Salt and freshly ground pepper
1 tomato, finely diced
3 scallions, thinly sliced

---

1. Heat oil in the pressure cooker. Add the celery, onion, hot peppers, garlic, and ham. Cook uncovered over medium-high heat until onions are translucent, 4 to 5 minutes. Add the black-eye peas, stock, and spice blend.

2. Cover and bring up to high pressure. Reduce heat to stabilize pressure and cook 10 minutes. Release pressure. Strain the solids from the liquid, reserving both. Transfer solids to a blender or food processor; add cilantro. Puree 2 minutes, adding a small amount of the reserved liquid if necessary to facilitate pureeing.

3. Transfer to a bowl and stir in the cooking liquid, half-and-half, and salt and pepper to taste. Garnish each serving with tomatoes and scallions. The soup thickens as it stands; if made in advance, it may need to be thinned with a little water or stock at serving time.

Black Bean Soup

There are almost as many versions of black bean soups as there are cooks. The best are simple and straightforward, as this one is. If you have a chipotle chile it can be added for a spicy bite.

Makes 6 to 8 servings

---

2 cups dried black beans, soaked
    overnight
3 ounces smoked slab bacon, finely
    diced
1 large onion, diced
2 jalapeño or serrano peppers, minced
1 tablespoon ground cumin

1 teaspoon ground coriander
1 can (16 ounces) diced tomatoes
4 to 5 cups Chicken Stock
    (page 25) or canned broth
1 cup sour cream
Salt and cayenne

---

1. Cook the bacon in the pressure cooker uncovered over medium heat until it begins to render its fat, about 3 minutes. Add the onion and hot peppers. Cook until the onion is tender, 7 to 9 minutes. Stir in the cumin and coriander and cook 1 minute. Add the tomatoes with their liquid, the beans and 4 cups of the stock or broth.

2. Cover the pressure cooker and bring up to high pressure. Reduce heat to stabilize pressure and cook 15 minutes. Release pressure naturally.

3. Carefully spoon 2 to 3 cups of the mixture into a blender or food processor and puree until smooth. Stir the puree back into soup along with the sour cream, salt, and cayenne. Add remaining stock if soup is too thick.

Italian Lentil Soup with Sausage and Peppers

Hearty soups, such as this one, keep the chill of winter at bay. If your pressure cooker is large enough, consider making a double recipe.

Makes 6 to 8 servings

---

1 tablespoon olive oil
½ pound Italian sausage, removed from casing
1 medium onion, chopped
1 medium red or green bell pepper, diced
2 celery ribs, diced
⅔ cup lentils

1 can (16 ounces) diced tomatoes
3 cups Chicken Stock (page 25) or canned broth
2 bay leaves
1 teaspoon dried basil
2 cups fresh spinach or Swiss chard leaves, sliced
Salt and freshly ground pepper

---

1. Heat the oil in the pressure cooker. Add the sausage and break into chunks. Add the onion, bell pepper, and celery. Cook uncovered over medium heat until sausage is cooked. Add lentils, tomatoes with their liquid, stock or broth, bay leaves, and basil.

2. Cover and bring up to high pressure. Reduce heat to stabilize pressure and cook 12 minutes. Release pressure. Add the spinach or chard. Season with salt and pepper to taste.

Peas, Please Soup

Fresh vegetables, including raw zucchini, add a welcome burst of freshness to split pea soup.

Makes 4 to 6 servings

---

2 ounces pancetta or smoked slab
  bacon, finely diced
1 tablespoon olive oil
1 celery rib, diced
1 small onion, diced
1 small parsnip, thinly sliced
1 cup dried split green peas

3 cups Chicken Stock (page 25),
  Vegetable Stock (page 24),
  or water
1 medium zucchini, very thinly sliced
3 tablespoons fresh basil leaves
1 cup half-and-half
Salt and freshly ground pepper

---

1. If using pancetta, heat the oil in the pressure cooker; bacon doesn't require any oil. Add pancetta or bacon and cook uncovered over medium heat until most of fat is rendered. Remove the cooked pancetta or bacon with a slotted spoon and set aside

2. Add the celery and onion to pan. Cook over medium heat until onion is translucent, 4 minutes. Stir in the parsnip, peas, and 2 cups of the stock. Cover the pressure cooker and bring up to high pressure. Reduce heat to stabilize pressure and cook 10 minutes. Release pressure naturally. Stir in zucchini.

3. Transfer the contents of cooker to a blender or food processor. Add basil and puree until smooth. Return to pressure cooker and stir in the remaining stock, half-and-half, reserved pancetta or bacon, and salt and pepper to taste. Heat gently to serving temperature.

Vegetable Stock

This recipe can be followed by the book or used as a guide for designing your own vegetable broth from ingredients on hand. Many vegetables can be used, but avoid strong-tasting ones such as turnips.

Makes 3 quarts

3 leeks, trimmed and cut into thirds	4 stems of parsley
3 carrots, cut into thirds	1 bay leaf
3 celery ribs, cut into thirds	4 whole peppercorns
1 large tomato, quartered	3 quarts water
1 small onion, halved	2 teaspoons white wine vinegar
2 whole garlic cloves, peeled	

1. Combine all ingredients in the pressure cooker. Cover and bring up to high pressure. Reduce heat to stabilize pressure and cook 12 minutes. Release pressure naturally.

2. Strain the stock, pressing on the vegetables to release as much flavor as possible. Refrigerate up to 4 days, or freeze.

Chicken Stock

Keep a collection of chicken bones, necks, backs, and wings in the freezer. When you have a good supply and some extra time on your hands, put together a rich stock.

Makes about 7 cups

2½ pounds chicken parts, such as
    bones, backs, wings, and necks
2 chicken feet (optional)
2 large carrots, cut into 1-inch pieces
1 large celery rib, cut into 1-inch
    pieces

1 medium onion, unpeeled, quartered
1 small leek or the green ends
    (optional)
4 whole peppercorns
8 cups water

---

1. Combine all ingredients in the pressure cooker. Cover and bring up to high pressure. Reduce heat to stabilize pressure and cook 25 minutes. Release pressure.
2. Strain the stock and refrigerate until the fat solidifies. Remove fat. Refrigerate up to 3 days, or freeze.

Beef Stock

Roasting the bones before cooking pays off with a richly flavored stock.

Makes about 6 cups

2½ pounds beef soup bones
1½ pounds beef shank bones
2 large carrots, cut into 1-inch pieces
2 celery ribs, cut into 1-inch pieces
1 large onion, unpeeled, quartered

4 sprigs parsley
6 whole peppercorns
1 bay leaf
7 cups water

---

1. Preheat oven to 450 degrees. Put bones and vegetables in a large shallow roasting pan. Roast in oven until the bones are browned, about 30 minutes.

2. Transfer the contents of roasting pan to the pressure cooker. Add the parsley, peppercorns, bay leaf, and water, making sure water does not exceed maximum amount for your cooker. Cover and bring up to high pressure. Reduce heat to stabilize pressure and cook 1¼ hours. Release pressure.

3. Strain the stock and refrigerate until the fat solidifies. Remove and discard fat. To make demiglace, boil the stock, uncovered, until it is reduced by half or more. Stock can be refrigerated up to 3 days, or frozen.

Ham Stock

Often overlooked in classical cooking, ham stock is a sturdy and flavorful base for soups, bean dishes, and stews. It can be refrigerated for up to 3 days or frozen for up to 2 months.

Makes 6 cups

---

2 smoked or fresh ham hocks or 1
   meaty ham bone
1 medium leek, well rinsed
1 medium onion, cut in half
1 large carrot, quartered
1 large tomato, cut in half

1 large celery rib, quartered
7 cups water
4 allspice berries
2 whole cloves
2 bay leaves

---

1. Combine all ingredients in the pressure cooker. Cover and bring up to high pressure. Reduce heat to stabilize pressure and cook 25 minutes.
2. Release pressure. Strain out the vegetables and degrease the stock. Cut meat from hocks or bone and reserve for another use.

Fish Stock

Fish frames often can be had just for asking the fishmonger. Many types work but avoid frames from oily fish, such as salmon and bluefish. A distinct advantage to using the pressure cooker is that the aroma is fairly well contained in the cooker.

Makes about 5 cups

---

1 tablespoon olive oil	4 cups water
1 medium leek, sliced	1 cup dry white wine
1 small onion, sliced	1 tablespoon white wine vinegar
2 large shallots, minced	4 sprigs parsley
2 tomatoes, chopped	1 branch fresh thyme, if available
2 pounds fish frames and heads, gills removed	

---

1. Heat the oil in the pressure cooker. Add the leek, onion, shallots, and tomatoes. Cook gently 5 minutes. Wrap the fish parts in cheesecloth and add to the cooker along with the water, wine, vinegar, parsley, and thyme.

2. Cover and bring up to high pressure. Reduce heat to stabilize pressure and cook 15 minutes. Release pressure. Discard the cheesecloth containing fish. Strain the stock through a fine strainer and refrigerate for up to 2 days, or freeze.

Poultry and Meat

With its reputation so solidly built on long-simmering soups and kettles of stews, it comes as something of a surprise to learn how deftly the pressure cooker performs its magic on simple cuts of meat and poultry. Pork chops, veal steaks, and chicken all cook in minutes. Boneless chicken breasts, wrapped in parchment, mimic a classic French preparation. Meatballs don't require the initial browning and cook right along with a sauce—all in less than 10 minutes.

Inexpensive, flavorful cuts of meat, such as shanks and pot roasts, have all but disappeared from many cooks' menus because they take so long to cook. Not true in the pressure cooker. Minutes rather than hours tame such cuts into tasty, meltingly tender delicacies worthy of any table.

The recipes that follow will increase the uses for your pressure cooker. Instead of relegating it to those times when you're preparing traditional, slow-simmering foods, think of your pressure cooker as a tool for all types of cooking.

Things to keep in mind:
- Removing the skin from cut-up chicken when cooking it in the pressure cooker is an excellent option that saves on fat and calories. The chicken will turn out especially flavorful since the

sauce it cooks in will be absorbed readily into the meat and will help to keep it moist.

- Tough cuts of meat often have a lot of fat. Cook them the day before, then refrigerate them so the fat can be skimmed from the surface of the sauce. For same-day serving, use a gravy strainer.
- Although browning meat in oil as a preliminary step adds flavor, it can be eliminated if you want to save on fat calories.
- After you remove meats from the pressure cooker, the pan juices can be boiled to thicken them and intensify flavors.
- If your cooker has variable settings, use lower pressure for chicken.

Farmhouse Chicken Fricassee

The pleasures of Sunday suppers are captured in this homey chicken and vegetable stew. If you have some extra time, homemade herbed buttermilk biscuits are just the right accompaniment, along with rice or pasta.

Makes 3 to 4 servings

1 tablespoon unsalted butter
1½ teaspoons vegetable oil
1 (3½-pound) chicken, cut in serving
  pieces
½ teaspoon salt
¼ teaspoon freshly ground pepper
3 medium carrots, cut in 1-inch pieces
2 celery ribs, cut in 1-inch pieces

1 small onion, cut in 4 to 6 wedges
2 tablespoons all-purpose flour
1 cup Chicken Stock (page 25) or
  canned broth
1 teaspoon dried marjoram
1 tablespoon minced fresh chives or
  parsley

1. Melt the butter with the oil in the pressure cooker. Add the chicken, in batches as necessary, and season with salt and pepper. Cook uncovered over medium heat, turning, until browned well on both sides, 5 to 7 minutes per batch. Carefully pour off all but 1 tablespoon fat. Add the carrots, celery, and onion. Sprinkle on flour and stir in. Cook, stirring, 1 to 2 minutes. Add stock or broth and marjoram.

2. Cover and bring to low pressure. Reduce heat to stabilize pressure and cook 12 minutes. (If your cooker has a fixed pressure regulating weight, cook at high pressure for 9 minutes.) Release pressure. Transfer the chicken and vegetables to a platter. Garnish with the minced chives. Skim the fat from the pan juices and pass separately to spoon over the chicken and vegetables.

Chicken with Leeks and Mustard Cream Sauce

Casual French bistro-style dining comes to mind with this simple chicken dish.

Makes 3 to 4 servings

---

2 strips of smoked bacon, diced
1 (3½-pound) chicken, cut in serving pieces
2 large shallots, minced
½ cup dry white wine
1 teaspoon dried rosemary
1 cup Chicken Stock (page 25) or canned broth

2 medium leeks (white and tender green), cut in 1-inch pieces
2 teaspoons Dijon mustard
¼ cup whipping cream
Salt and freshly ground pepper

---

1. Cook the bacon in the pressure cooker uncovered over medium heat until browned, 3 to 5 minutes. Remove with a slotted spoon and set aside. Add the chicken, in batches without crowding, and cook, turning until nicely browned, 5 to 7 minutes per batch. Set chicken aside as it is browned. Add the shallots to pan and cook 1 minute. Add the wine and rosemary. Boil until wine is reduced by half, about 2 minutes. Return the chicken and bacon to the cooker. Add the stock or broth and scatter leeks over the chicken.

2. Cover and bring to low pressure. Reduce heat to stabilize pressure and cook 10 minutes. (If your cooker has a fixed pressure regulating weight, cook at high pressure for 7 minutes.) Release pressure.

3. Remove the chicken and leeks; set aside, covered to keep warm. Whisk mustard into pan juices and boil over high heat until reduced by about one-third, 2 to 3 minutes. Add the cream and continue boiling until the sauce is thickened, about 3 minutes. Season with salt and pepper to taste and pour sauce over the chicken and leeks.

Garlic Lemon Chicken

Many Chicagoans are well acquainted with a local favorite known as chicken Vesuvio. In its best form, it is a garlicky chicken and potato dish baked with lemon and wine. Here, the cooking method has changed, though the end result is just as satisfying.

Makes 4 servings

¼ cup olive oil
1 (3½-pound) chicken, cut into serving pieces
½ teaspoon salt
¼ teaspoon freshly ground pepper
6 small red potatoes, halved
3 to 4 large garlic cloves, minced

½ cup dry white wine
¼ cup Chicken Stock (page 25) or
  canned broth
Juice and finely grated zest of 1 lemon
1 teaspoon dried oregano
Pinch of crushed hot pepper flakes
3 tablespoons minced fresh parsley

---

1. Heat the oil in the pressure cooker. Add the chicken and season with salt and pepper. Cook over medium heat, turning, until chicken is well browned, 5 to 7 minutes. Add the potatoes, ¾ of the garlic, the wine, stock or broth, lemon juice, oregano, and hot pepper.

2. Cover and bring to low pressure. Reduce heat to stabilize pressure and cook 16 minutes. (If your cooker has a fixed pressure regulating weight, cook at high pressure for 12 minutes.) Release pressure.

3. Remove the chicken to a platter and keep warm. Leave the potatoes in the cooker but turn them so cut sides are down. Boil over high heat until the juices are reduced by about half, 5 to 7 minutes. Season the sauce with additional salt and pepper to taste.

4. Combine the remaining garlic, lemon zest and parsley. Arrange the potatoes around chicken, pour the sauce over all, and sprinkle parsley mixture on top.

Chicken Breasts with Tomatoes, Basil, and Goat Cheese

Cooking chicken in parchment packets is part of the French culinary tradition. The breasts are tender and moist and are finished off with a summery topping. Feta cheese can be used in place of the goat cheese.

Makes 2 servings

---

2 teaspoons olive oil (basil- or garlic-flavored, if available)

1 teaspoon balsamic vinegar

½ teaspoon Dijon mustard

2 skinned and boned chicken breast halves

Salt and freshly ground pepper

2 small plum tomatoes, diced

2 tablespoons minced fresh basil

2 tablespoons crumbled goat cheese

---

1. Combine the oil, vinegar, and mustard in a small dish; set aside. Gently flatten the chicken breasts so they are uniformly thick. Season lightly with salt and pepper. Fold in half 2 sheets of paper about 15 inches square; open up and place flat on the counter with fold lying horizontally. Place a chicken breast half just above the fold on each sheet. Sprinkle the tomatoes and half the basil over chicken and drizzle oil mixture over all.

2. Fold and crimp the packets to form half-moons. Close them so they are airtight; seal with paper clips, if necessary.

3. Put steamer insert in pressure cooker with 1½ cups water. Arrange packets on steamer. Cover the pressure cooker and bring up to high pressure. Reduce heat to stabilize pressure and cook 8 minutes. Release pressure. Transfer the packets to serving plates and carefully open. Sprinkle the goat cheese and remaining basil on top of chicken and serve.

Honey Mustard Chicken Breasts
with Carrots and Leeks

Here julienned vegetables steam right along with chicken in parchment envelopes. For convenience, the packets can be assembled ahead of time and refrigerated until you're ready to cook them.

Makes 2 servings

---

1 tablespoon unsalted butter, melted

1 tablespoon honey mustard

½ teaspoon curry powder

2 skinned and boned chicken breast halves

Salt and freshly ground pepper

1 small leek (white part only), cut in thin strips

1 small carrot, cut in thin strips

1 tablespoon minced fresh parsley

---

1. Combine the butter, mustard, and curry powder in a small dish. Gently flatten the chicken breasts so they are uniformly thick. Season lightly with salt and pepper. Fold in half 2 sheets of parchment paper 15 inches square; open and place flat on the counter with fold lying horizontally. Place a chicken breast half just above the fold on each sheet. Sprinkle the leek, carrot, and parsley over chicken. Spread the butter mixture on top.

2. Fold and crimp the packets to form half-moons. Close them so they are airtight; use paper clips, if necessary.

3. Put steamer insert in pressure cooker and add 1½ cups water. Arrange packets on steamer. Cover the pressure cooker and bring up to low pressure. Reduce heat to stabilize pressure and cook 10 minutes. Release pressure. Transfer packets to serving plates.

Poached Chicken Plus Stock

The uses for poached chicken are seemingly endless, making this easy preparation a valuable one. After the chicken is cooked, a simple stock awaits, which can be used at once, refrigerated for up to 3 days, or frozen for up to 2 months.

Makes 2 to 3 servings

1 (3-pound) whole chicken
1 small onion, quartered
1 carrot, cut in 1-inch pieces
2 celery ribs, cut in 1-inch pieces

1 tomato, quartered
2 sprigs of parsley
3 whole black peppercorns
6 cups water

1. Combine all ingredients in the pressure cooker. Cover and bring up to low pressure. Reduce heat to stabilize pressure and cook 12 minutes. (If your cooker has a fixed pressure regulating weight, cook at high pressure for 9 minutes.) Turn off heat. Leave the pressure cooker locked for 35 to 40 minutes.

2. When chicken is cool enough to handle, remove the meat from the bones. Discard skin; return bones to the liquid in the pan.

3. Cover and bring up to high pressure. Reduce heat to stabilize pressure and cook 20 minutes. Release pressure. Strain stock. Refrigerate until the fat solidifies. Skim off fat before using.

Stuffed Cabbage Rolls

Ground turkey, a lower-fat alternative to ground beef, is a satisfying filling for cabbage rolls when flavored with sweet nuggets of prunes and bits of greens.

Makes 4 to 6 servings

---

10 to 12 large cabbage leaves, plus
    1 cup finely chopped green cabbage
1 tablespoon vegetable oil
1 medium onion, chopped
2 cups finely chopped Swiss chard
1 pound ground turkey
½ cup pitted prunes, finely chopped
1 large egg

1 slice of firm-textured white bread,
    finely crumbled
1 teaspoon salt
⅛ teaspoon ground allspice
⅛ teaspoon freshly ground pepper
1 can (16 ounces) stewed tomatoes
½ cup Chicken Stock (page 25) or
    canned broth

---

1. In a large saucepan of boiling salted water, cook the whole cabbage leaves until slightly translucent and pliable, 6 to 8 minutes. Drain and rinse briefly under cold water. Pat dry.

2. Heat the oil in the pressure cooker over medium heat. Add the onion, chard, and chopped cabbage. Cook uncovered, stirring often, until tender, 4 to 5 minutes. Transfer to a large bowl and add the ground turkey, prunes, egg, bread, salt, allspice, and pepper; mix well. Using ⅓ to ½ cup filling for each, spoon the mixture onto the cabbage leaves. Bring up the stem ends, fold in sides, and roll into packets.

3. Combine tomatoes and stock or broth in the pressure cooker. Add cabbage rolls, seam side down. Cover and bring up to high pressure. Reduce heat to stabilize pressure and cook 8 minutes. Release pressure. Serve cabbage rolls with sauce spooned on top.

Texas Ranch-style Brisket

A dry rub marinade infuses this brisket with a spicy edge that is picked up again in the simple sauce. Start this dish two to three days before you plan to serve it because it marinates for a day or two, and the best strategy is to cook the meat a day or two ahead, so excess fat can be skimmed from the sauce.

Makes 6 to 8 servings

1 small onion, minced
2 large garlic cloves, minced
1 serrano pepper, seeded and minced
1½ tablespoons brown sugar
1 tablespoon mild pure ground chile
1 tablespoon cider vinegar
½ teaspoon ground cumin

½ teaspoon salt
1 small beef brisket, about 3 pounds
1½ tablespoons vegetable oil
1 can (10 ounces) diced tomatoes with chiles
1 medium onion, cut in 6 to 8 wedges

1. Combine onion, garlic, serrano pepper, brown sugar, ground chile, vinegar, cumin, and salt in a small dish. Rub the mixture over both sides of the brisket. Place the meat in a glass baking dish, cover, and refrigerate 24 to 36 hours.

2. Heat the oil in the pressure cooker. When it is hot, add meat and cook uncovered over medium-high heat, turning once, until brown on both sides, 6 to 8 minutes. Add tomatoes with their liquid, lifting the meat so the tomatoes cover the bottom of the pan. Scatter the onion wedges on top.

3. Cover and bring up to high pressure. Reduce heat to stabilize pressure and cook 1 hour. Release pressure. To serve, skim the fat from the pan juices. Slice the meat across the grain and serve with the pan juices.

Korean-style Pot Roast

Beef chuck, which is an inexpensive cut of meat, has a rich flavor and natural succulence when it is cooked in a pressure cooker. There are many ways to season and serve it, but this Korean-inspired sauce offers an unusual alternative to some of the more familiar recipes.

Makes 4 to 6 servings

---

3 garlic cloves

2 jalapeño or serrano peppers, seeded
   if desired

2 tablespoons brown sugar

2½ tablespoons Asian sesame oil

2 tablespoons hoisin sauce

1 tablespoon fresh lime juice

½ teaspoon salt

½ teaspoon coarsely cracked black
   pepper

2 pounds boneless beef chuck roast

¾ cup Beef Stock (page 26) or
   canned broth

2 large carrots, peeled and cut in 1½-
   inch lengths

2 large celery ribs, cut in 1½-inch
   lengths

2 scallions, bias-cut in 1-inch pieces

---

1. Mince the garlic and hot peppers. Sprinkle on the sugar and, using the flat side of a large knife, smash the mixture into a paste. Transfer to a small dish and add 1½ tablespoons of the sesame oil, the hoisin sauce, lime juice, salt, and pepper. Reserve half of the paste; spread the remaining paste over both sides of the roast, cover, and refrigerate 4 to 12 hours.

2. Heat the remaining 1 tablespoon sesame oil in the pressure cooker over medium-high heat. Add the roast and cook uncovered, turning once, until brown on both sides, 6 to 8 minutes. Add the stock or broth.

---

3. Cover and bring up to high pressure. Reduce heat to stabilize pressure and cook 20 minutes. Release pressure by running cold water over the cover. Add the carrots and celery. Return to high pressure; reduce heat to stabilize pressure, and cook 10 minutes. Release pressure.

4. Transfer meat and vegetables to a serving platter. Top with scallions and season with additional salt and pepper to taste. Tent with foil to keep warm. Skim the fat from the pan juices and return juices to the pressure cooker. Add reserved seasoning paste mixture. Boil over high heat until reduced to about 1 cup, about 10 minutes. Moisten meat and vegetables with some of the sauce and pass the rest separately.

County Cork Corned Beef

This is a fine feast in the best Irish tradition. Cabbage and potatoes are the usual choices, but turnips, carrots, and rutabaga all are wonderful additions as well.

Makes 6 to 8 servings

---

4 pounds corned brisket of beef
1 head of garlic, cut in half crosswise
1 onion, quartered
2 tablespoons pickling spice
5 whole black peppercorns
3 whole allspice berries
2 tablespoons cider vinegar

1 head of green cabbage, cut in 8 wedges
6 to 8 small red potatoes, peeled and halved
Horseradish or horseradish sauce, for serving

---

1. Place the brisket in the pressure cooker and cover with cold water, making sure the amount does not exceed the recommended level for your cooker. Add the garlic, onion, pickling spice, peppercorns, allspice, and vinegar.

2. Cover and bring up to high pressure. Reduce heat to stabilize pressure and cook 60 minutes. Release pressure and remove meat.

3. Add the cabbage and potatoes to the cooker and bring up to high pressure. As soon as high pressure is reached, release pressure. Serve the meat in thin slices along with the vegetables. Pass the horseradish on the side.

Pot Roast with Farm Vegetables

Trend watchers say homespun recipes like this are back in style. Good cooks know they were never gone.

Makes 4 to 6 servings

---

1 tablespoon vegetable oil
2 pounds boneless beef chuck roast
2 onions, 1 large and 1 small
3 celery ribs, bias-cut in 1-inch pieces
3 carrots, peeled and bias-cut in
   1-inch pieces
1 parsnip, peeled and sliced
2 bay leaves

2 teaspoons paprika
½ teaspoon salt
¼ teaspoon freshly ground pepper
1 cup diced tomatoes, fresh or canned
¾ cup Beef Stock (page 26) or
   canned broth
2 medium red potatoes, cut lengthwise
   into 4 wedges each

---

1. Heat the oil in the pressure cooker over medium-high heat. Add the roast and cook uncovered, turning until brown, 6 to 8 minutes. Chop the small onion and add it to the cooker along with 1 celery rib, 1 carrot, the parsnip, bay leaves, paprika, salt, and pepper.

2. Cover and bring up to high pressure. Reduce heat to stabilize pressure and cook 25 minutes. Release pressure; remove meat and set aside, covered, to keep warm. Skin the fat from pan juices and remove the bay leaves. Puree the juices and cooked vegetables in a blender or food processor.

3. Return the puree to the cooker. Cut remaining onion into wedges and add to the pan along with the remaining celery and carrots. Cover the pressure cooker and bring up to high pressure. Reduce heat to stabilize pressure and cook 6 minutes. Release pressure. Serve the meat in thin slices, surrounded by vegetables and topped with the sauce.

Pork Chops with Tomato Relish

A Southern tradition of marinating pork in buttermilk is used as a prelude to an Italian cooking style.

Makes 4 servings

---

4 center-cut pork chops, cut ½ inch thick, well trimmed
⅔ cup buttermilk
2 tablespoons olive oil
1 medium onion, cut in wedges
1 green bell pepper, cut in 1-inch strips
1 to 2 small dried red chiles

2 tablespoons chopped fresh basil or ½ teaspoon dried basil
1 tablespoon balsamic or red wine vinegar
1 can (16 ounces) ready-cut diced tomatoes
Salt and freshly ground pepper

---

1. Marinate the pork chops in buttermilk for 4 to 6 hours before cooking. Drain and pat dry.

2. Heat oil in the pressure cooker over high heat. Brown the pork chops well on both sides; set aside. Add the onion, bell pepper, dried chiles, and dried basil to cooker. Cook, stirring often, until onions begin to brown at the edges, 4 to 5 minutes. Pour in the vinegar, then add the tomatoes and their juice. Arrange the pork chops over the top.

3. Cover and bring up to low pressure. Reduce heat to stabilize pressure and cook 15 minutes. Release pressure. Season the sauce with salt and pepper to taste. Add fresh basil if using. Serve the pork chops with the sauce spooned over them.

Teriyaki-Glazed Ribs

These bronze beauties proved to be one of the most popular recipes from my first pressure cooker book, a surefire bet to show up at barbecues, picnics, and parties all summer long. The cooking is a two-step process. Ribs are parcooked in the pressure cooker, bathed in a savory marinade, then finished to perfection on the grill.

Makes 3 to 4 servings

---

3 pounds pork spareribs
½ cup light brown sugar
⅓ cup soy sauce

⅓ cup ketchup
⅓ cup hoisin sauce

---

1. Cut the ribs into pieces of about 4 ribs each. Place in the pressure cooker and add water to cover, making sure the water doesn't go beyond maximum fill level. Cover and bring up to high pressure. Reduce heat to stabilize pressure and cook 12 minutes. Release, drain ribs, and allow to cool slightly.

2. In a large bowl, combine the brown sugar, soy sauce, ketchup, and hoisin sauce. Stir to mix well. Add ribs and turn to coat. Cover and refrigerate 12 to 24 hours.

3. Prepare a medium-hot grill, preferably with a mix of charcoal and wood. Remove the ribs from the marinade, letting excess marinade drip back into bowl. When coals are ashy, add the ribs. Grill until they are browned on both sides, brushing them several times with reserved marinade.

Pulled Pork Sandwiches

The best pulled pork sandwiches are those discovered on the barbecue trail in South Carolina. Short of that, this recipe offers a fine taste of the tangy, meltingly tender pork, which some say makes the best sandwiches ever. A traditional adjunct is vinegary cole slaw served atop the pork.

Makes 6 servings

---

1 boneless pork loin roast, about 3 pounds	½ teaspoon freshly ground pepper
	1¼ cups cider vinegar
1½ tablespoons sugar	¼ to ⅓ cup smoky barbecue sauce
½ teaspoon salt	6 toasted hamburger buns

---

1. Put the pork roast in the pressure cooker. Sprinkle sugar, salt, and pepper over the meat. Add vinegar.

2. Cover and bring up to high pressure. Reduce heat to stabilize pressure and cook for 45 minutes. Release pressure.

3. Transfer the pork to a bowl. When it is cool enough to handle, shred the meat with two forks. Skim the fat from the pan juices and add about 2 tablespoons of the skimmed juices to meat. Mix well. Add just enough barbecue sauce to moisten and flavor meat. Serve warm on toasted buns.

Provençal Lamb Shanks with White Beans

Flavorful lamb shanks are often pushed aside in favor of cuts that cook more quickly. In the pressure cooker, they become meltingly tender and succulent in less than 30 minutes.

Makes 2 servings

⅓ cup navy pea beans, soaked
    overnight
1½ tablespoons olive oil
2 small lamb shanks, about 12 ounces
    each
½ teaspoon salt
¼ teaspoon freshly ground pepper
4 large garlic cloves, peeled and left
    whole

1 small onion, chopped
1 can (16 ounces) diced tomatoes
½ cup Chicken Stock (page 25) or
    canned broth
1 teaspoon dried sage
2 tablespoons minced fresh basil or
    parsley

1. Heat the oil in the pressure cooker over high heat. Add the lamb shanks and season with the salt and pepper. Cook uncovered, turning, 3 minutes. Add the garlic and onion and cook, continuing to turn shanks, until they are well browned and onions are tender, 3 to 5 minutes longer. Add the tomatoes with their liquid, the stock or broth, and sage. Drain beans and add to pot.
2. Cover and bring up to high pressure. Reduce heat to stabilize pressure and cook 25 minutes. Release pressure. Add basil or parsley, season with additional salt and pepper to taste, and serve.

Veal Shanks Milanese

Also called osso buco, this is a splendid dish of long-simmered veal shanks in a thick, rich broth. It is traditionally served with risotto, but also goes well with soft polenta or penne pasta.

Makes 2 servings

---

2 tablespoons olive oil
2 pounds veal shanks, cut into 2-inch
  pieces
1 large carrot, finely diced
1 large celery rib, finely diced
1 small onion, cut in 8 wedges
1½ tablespoons all-purpose flour
2 large garlic cloves, minced
½ cup dry white wine
½ cup Chicken Stock (page 25) or
  canned broth

1 cup diced fresh or canned tomatoes,
  well drained
1 teaspoon dried basil
2 tablespoons minced fresh parsley
2 teaspoons grated lemon zest
2 to 3 teaspoons balsamic vinegar
Salt
¼ teaspoon freshly ground pepper

---

1. Heat the oil in the pressure cooker over high heat. Add the shanks and cook uncovered, until browned well on one side, 4 to 5 minutes. Turn shanks over and sprinkle the carrot, celery, and onion over the shanks. Cook until the other side is browned, about 4 minutes longer. Sprinkle the flour over the surface and stir in. Add half the garlic and cook 30 seconds. Add the wine and boil until almost all of the wine has evaporated, 4 to 5 minutes. Add the stock or broth, tomatoes, and basil.

2. Cover and bring up to high pressure. Reduce heat to stabilize pressure and cook 20 minutes. Release pressure.

3. Meanwhile, make a *gremolata* by combining the remaining garlic with the parsley, and lemon zest in a small dish; set aside.

4. Skim fat from the surface of the sauce and add vinegar, salt, and pepper. Serve the shanks with *gremolata* sprinkled over top.

Veal Steaks with Mixed Pepper Compote

Veal steaks adapt well to quick cooking. Pork steaks can also be used in this preparation that pairs the meat with a colorful sweet bell pepper topping.

Makes 4 servings

1½ tablespoons olive oil
1 small garlic clove, minced
3 small bell peppers, preferably 1 each red, yellow, and green, cut in ¾-inch strips
1 small red onion, cut in 4 to 6 wedges
¼ teaspoon dried thyme
½ teaspoon salt

¼ teaspoon freshly ground pepper
1 medium tomato, halved, seeded, and cut in thin strips
1½ tablespoons unsalted butter
2 veal steaks, 8 to 10 ounces each
½ cup dry white wine or dry vermouth
⅓ cup Chicken Stock (page 25) or canned broth
1 tablespoon tomato paste

---

1. Heat the oil in the pressure cooker over high heat. Stir in the garlic and cook uncovered 30 seconds. Add the bell peppers, red onion, thyme, salt, and pepper. Cook, stirring often, until peppers begin to brown, 3 to 4 minutes. Remove from cooker. Add tomato strips to vegetables and set aside.

2. Return cooker to high heat and add half the butter. When it is melted, add veal. Brown on both sides. Add wine, stock, and tomato paste.

3. Cover and bring up to high pressure. Reduce heat to stabilize pressure and cook 4 minutes. Release pressure by running cold water over the lid. Add vegetable mixture, return to high pressure, and cook 2 minutes.

4. Remove meat and vegetables from pan. Boil juices 2 minutes; whisk in remaining butter. Season with additional salt and pepper to taste, pour over meat and vegetables, and serve.

Fish and Seafood

One of the most appealing—and amazing—things about the pressure cooker is the breadth of uses it has. Unlike other more limited appliances, it cooks many types and styles of food very well. And while its skill with a soup or a stew and the ability to turn tough into tender are pretty widely acclaimed, its finesse with fish and seafood is somewhat unexpected. Along with all the other culinary accomplishments claimed by pressure cooking, preparing seafood is yet another feather in the cap.

By their nature, these bounteous offerings from the waters cook quickly no matter what method is used. But quick or not, cooks often are wary of preparing fish at home. Even though Americans are eating more seafood than ever before, fish is still not enjoyed with the same familiarity as meat and poultry. While a cook may be able to rattle off a dozen or so ways to make chicken, fewer top-of-the-head fish recipes come to mind. And then there's the seemingly endless struggle with overcooked or undercooked.

Fish in the pressure cooker can be explored by novices and skilled cooks alike. From perfectly steamed mussels to delicate and aromatic packets of fish and vegetables, from light fish soups to rich, creamy chowders, the pressure cooker is an assured option.

Hints and tips:

- For best results with fish fillets and fish steaks, don't have them cut more than ½ to ¾ inch thick.
- Time carefully. It is better to undercook than overcook, since you can always add more time if the fish isn't cooked to your liking.
- Fish with delicate flesh, such as walleye pike and sole, are best used in soups or stews in the pressure cooker. Cooked as fillets, they tend to break apart.

Chinese Steamed Fish and Vegetables

Colorful and light, this Oriental entree can be made without any oil for a fat-free alternative.

Makes 2 servings

2 cod fillets, about 6 ounces each
¼ cup fresh snow peas, cut on diagonal into ¾-inch slices
½ of a small red bell pepper, cut in thin strips
1 slice of fresh ginger, about the size of a quarter, slivered

2 scallions, sliced
1 teaspoon chili oil or Asian sesame oil
Salt
1½ tablespoons seasoned rice vinegar
3 tablespoons minced cilantro or parsley

1. Fold in half 2 sheets of parchment paper 15 inches square. Open flat on the counter, with fold horizontal. Place a piece of fish on each, just above the fold. Scatter the snow peas, bell pepper, ginger, and scallions over fish. Drizzle on oil and season with salt to taste.

2. Fold and crimp the packets to form half-moons. Seal them so they are airtight; use paper clips, if necessary.

3. Put the steamer insert in the pressure cooker and add 1½ cups water. Place the packets on the steamer insert. Cover the pressure cooker and bring up to high pressure. Reduce heat to stabilize pressure and cook 6 minutes. Release pressure by running cold water over lid. Transfer the packets to a serving plate. Open carefully. Drizzle vinegar over fish and garnish with cilantro or parsley.

Bouillabaisse Marseilles

This French Provençal soup combines a richly flavored broth with a mix of fresh seafood. A selection of several types is most authentic. Several varieties of firm, white-fleshed fish and shellfish will contribute a more complex flavor to the dish.

Makes 4 servings

3 tablespoons olive oil

1 medium leek, white part only, sliced

1 medium onion, sliced

1 small fennel bulb, thinly sliced (or use celery and add ¾ teaspoon fennel seed to bouquet garni)

2 large garlic cloves, minced

1 cup dry white wine

1 strip of orange zest, about 3 inches long, removed with a vegetable peeler

3 cups Fish Stock (page 28) or bottled clam juice

4 large tomatoes, peeled, seeded, and finely chopped

1 bouquet garni made with 2 bay leaves, dried thyme, dried marjoram, and a sprig of parsley

Pinch of saffron threads

Pinch of cayenne

¾ pound halibut or monkfish fillets

1 lobster tail (optional)

6 ounces shelled and deveined large shrimp

6 ounces scallops

Salt and freshly ground pepper

1. Heat the oil in the pressure cooker over medium-low heat. Add the leek, onion, fennel, and garlic. Cook until softened, 6 to 7 minutes. Increase heat to high. Add the wine and orange zest and heat to a boil. Add fish stock, tomatoes, bouquet garni, saffron, and cayenne.

2. Cover and bring up to high pressure. Reduce heat to stabilize pressure and cook 5 minutes.

3. While broth is cooking, cut fish fillets and lobster into 1-inch pieces. Leave shrimp and scallops whole.

4. Release pressure and add fish and shellfish. Bring up to low pressure and remove from heat. Release pressure and remove orange zest and bouquet garni. Season with salt and pepper to taste and serve.

Down East Scallop and Leek Chowder

Elegant and light, this can be served as a prelude to a formal meal, or it can anchor a Sunday supper.

Makes 4 servings

2 tablespoons unsalted butter

1 jalapeño or serrano pepper, seeded and minced

1 garlic clove, minced

½ teaspoon minced fresh ginger

2 medium red potatoes, peeled and cut in ⅜-inch cubes

2 medium leeks (white and tender green), cut in ½-inch lengths

1 small red bell pepper, diced

½ cup dry white wine

2 cups Fish Stock (page 28) or 1 cup clam juice diluted with 1 cup water

1 teaspoon minced orange zest

1 pound sea scallops, cut crosswise in half

1 teaspoon minced fresh tarragon or ½ teaspoon dried

1 cup whipping cream

Salt and freshly ground pepper

1. Melt the butter in the pressure cooker. Add the hot pepper, garlic, and ginger. Cook uncovered over high heat, stirring, for 1 minute. Add the potatoes, leeks, and bell pepper. Mix well and cook 2 minutes. Add the wine; heat to a boil. Add the stock or clam juice and the orange zest.

2. Cover and bring up to high pressure. Reduce heat to stabilize pressure and cook 1 minute. Release pressure and add scallops and tarragon. Cook uncovered over medium-low heat just until scallops are cooked, 45 seconds. Add the cream and season with salt and pepper to taste. Serve at once.

San Francisco Fish Soup

Many cuisines have their own renditions of fish soup. This soup borrows most liberally from cioppino, which is often associated with San Francisco.

Makes 4 servings

1½ tablespoons olive oil
2 garlic cloves, minced
1 small onion, chopped
½ of a small fennel bulb or 1 large celery rib, finely diced
1 strip of orange zest, about 3 inches long, removed with a vegetable peeler
3 bay leaves
1 teaspoon dried tarragon
1 cup dry white wine

1 bottle (8 ounces) clam juice or 1 cup Fish Stock (page 28)
1 can (8 ounces) tomato sauce
12 mussels, scrubbed
½ pound bay scallops
½ pound shelled and deveined medium shrimp
1 fillet firm-fleshed white fish, such as halibut, cut in 1-inch cubes
Salt and freshly ground pepper
¼ cup chopped fresh basil

---

1. Heat the oil in the pressure cooker. Add the garlic, onion, and fennel or celery. Cook uncovered over medium heat until they begin to soften, about 4 minutes. Add orange zest, bay leaves, and tarragon; cook 30 seconds. Add wine and heat to a boil. Boil 1 minute. Add clam juice or stock and tomato sauce.

2. Cover and bring up to high pressure. Reduce heat to stabilize pressure and cook 5 minutes. Release pressure by running cold water over the lid. Add shellfish and fish. Return cover and lock into place. Bring up to low pressure. Release pressure with cold water. Remove orange zest and bay leaves. Season with salt and pepper to taste, add basil, and serve.

Mussel Stew with Chipotle Chile

Speed is not the overwhelming advantage when cooking mussels in the pressure cooker, although it is quick. The big bonus is that the aroma from cooking stays tightly contained in the cooker.

Makes 2 to 4 servings

---

1 tablespoon unsalted butter

1 medium onion, diced

2 small red potatoes, cut in ¼-inch dice

½ to 1 canned chipotle chile, minced (or use a dried, soaked chipotle)

1 cup Fish Stock (page 28) or clam juice

2 medium tomatoes, peeled, seeded, and finely diced

2 pounds mussels, scrubbed and debearded

3 tablespoons sour cream

½ cup chopped fresh cilantro, plus additional leaves for garnish

Salt

---

1. Melt the butter in the pressure cooker. Add the onion and potatoes. Cook uncovered over medium-high heat until the onion begins to soften, about 3 minutes. Add the chipotle chile and cook 30 seconds. Add stock or clam juice and tomatoes. Bring to a boil, then add the mussels.

2. Cover and bring up to high pressure over high heat. As soon as high pressure is reached, remove from heat. Release pressure by running cold water over the cover. With a slotted spoon, transfer the mussels to serving bowls.

3. Boil the contents of the cooker over high heat for 2 minutes. Remove from heat and whisk in sour cream. Add chopped cilantro and season with salt if needed. Pour over the mussels and garnish with cilantro leaves.

Caribbean Pork with Sweet Potatoes

A mix of sweet and hot flavors in a citrusy base turns pork tenderloin into a sassy stew.

Makes 3 to 4 servings

---

1 tablespoon vegetable oil
1 medium onion, cut in ½-inch wedges
⅛ to ¼ teaspoon cayenne
Pinch of ground allspice
1 pound pork tenderloin, cut in 1-inch cubes
2 medium sweet potatoes, cut in 1-inch chunks

1 medium green bell pepper, cut in 1-inch squares
½ cup orange juice
½ cup Chicken Stock (page 25) or canned broth
1 tablespoon soy sauce
1 teaspoon honey
1 teaspoon grated orange zest
Salt and freshly ground pepper

---

1. Heat the oil in the pressure cooker over high heat. Add the onion, cayenne, and allspice. Cook, stirring often, until onion begins to brown at the edges, about 4 minutes. Add the meat and cook, turning, until well browned. Add the sweet potatoes, bell pepper, orange juice, stock or broth, soy sauce, and honey.
2. Cover the pressure cooker and bring up to low pressure. Reduce heat to stabilize pressure and cook 6 minutes. Release the pressure. Stir in the orange zest and season with salt and pepper to taste.

Malay Curried Pork and Potatoes

Malaysian cooking is marked by sophisticated and exotic blends of spices and aromatics. Here hot, sweet, and citric tastes combine in a richly flavored stew. The intensity of curry paste blends varies, so add it in small increments until the level of heat is just right.

Makes 4 servings

---

3 large shallots
2 large garlic cloves
1 piece of peeled fresh ginger, about
   ¾-inch cube
1 stalk of lemongrass (see Note),
   trimmed, tender part cut in 1-inch
   pieces
2 tablespoons vegetable oil
2 to 3 teaspoons prepared red curry
   paste

1 teaspoon sugar
½ teaspoon ground cardamom
½ teaspoon cinnamon
1¼ pounds pork stew meat, cut in
   1-inch cubes
6 small red new potatoes, cut in half
⅔ cup Chicken Stock (page 25) or
   canned broth
¼ cup coconut milk
Salt

---

1. Mince the shallots, garlic, ginger, and lemongrass to a fine pulp in a food processor or blender.

2. Heat the oil in the pressure cooker over medium heat. Add the minced shallot mixture, the curry paste, sugar, cardamom, and cinnamon. Cook uncovered, stirring occasionally, until the oil begins to separate out, about 5 minutes. Add the pork, raise the heat to high, and cook, turning, until the meat is no longer pink, about 5 minutes longer. Add the potatoes, stock or broth, and coconut milk.

3. Cover and bring up to high pressure. Reduce heat to stabilize pressure and cook 12 minutes. Release pressure and season with salt to taste.

NOTE: Lemongrass, a fragrant seasoning common to Asian cooking, is increasingly available at Asian markets and some large supermarkets. If it is not available, omit it.

Pozole

Tradition isn't strictly adhered to in this version of a Southwestern classic. Black beans are an updated addition that combines seamlessly with the rest of the stew.

Makes 6 servings

1¾ pounds country-style pork loin ribs
1 pound pork neck bones (optional)
3 to 4 dried ancho chiles
Stems from 1 bunch of cilantro
1¼ cups water
1 can (16 ounces) hominy, drained
1 can (15 or 16 ounces) black beans,
    rinsed and drained

3 scallions, sliced
2 large tomatoes, diced
1 jalapeño or serrano pepper, minced
Salt and freshly ground pepper
Chopped cilantro, for garnish

---

1. Combine the ribs, neck bones if using, ancho chiles, cilantro stems, and water in the pressure cooker. Cover and bring up to high pressure. Reduce heat to stabilize pressure and cook 15 minutes. Release pressure. When the ribs are cool enough to handle, remove them from the broth and shred the meat; discard bones. Strain and degrease broth.

2. Transfer the meat to the pressure cooker. Add hominy, black beans, scallions, tomatoes, hot pepper, and enough broth to make a thick stewlike soup. Heat gently. Season with salt and pepper to taste and garnish with cilantro.

Pork, Potato, and Sauerkraut Goulash

A Hungarian rhapsody is brought to the dinner table as a steaming stew. For a lighter rendition, the sour cream may be omitted, although it does meld all the flavors together in a wonderful way.

Makes 4 servings

---

2 tablespoons vegetable oil

1 medium onion, diced

1½ pounds lean pork shoulder, cut in 1-inch cubes

½ cup dry white wine or dry vermouth

2 tablespoons imported sweet paprika

½ cup Chicken Stock (page 25) or canned broth

2 medium red or yellow potatoes, cut in 1-inch chunks

1 cup sauerkraut, well rinsed

½ cup sour cream

1 medium tomato, diced

½ teaspoon salt

¼ teaspoon freshly ground pepper

---

1. Heat the oil in the pressure cooker. Add the onion and cook uncovered over medium-high heat until it is soft, about 4 minutes. Add the pork and cook, turning, until the surface is no longer pink, about 4 minutes longer. Pour in the wine and stir up any browned bits from the bottom of the pan.

2. Stir the paprika into the chicken stock. Add to the cooker along with the potatoes and sauerkraut. Cover and bring up to high pressure. Reduce heat to stabilize pressure and cook 12 minutes. Release pressure.

3. Stir in sour cream, tomato, salt, and pepper. Cook gently, uncovered, 1 minute.

Laredo Lamb and Potato Stew

Smoky Southwest flavors abound in this spicy stew. Canned chipotles are becoming more common in supermarkets and specialty markets. When you track them down, be sure to stock up. They add an unbeatable kick of heat and smoke to many dishes.

Makes 6 servings

---

2 tablespoons vegetable oil
1½ pounds lamb stew meat, cut in
   1-inch pieces
2 teaspoons ground cumin
½ teaspoon salt
¼ teaspoon freshly ground pepper
1 tablespoon cider vinegar
2 medium sweet potatoes, scrubbed, cut
   in 1-inch chunks

2 medium red potatoes, scrubbed, cut
   in 1-inch chunks
1 small onion, cut in ½-inch wedges
3 tablespoons all-purpose flour
¾ cup beer
½ to 1 canned chipotle chile in adobo
   sauce, mashed
1½ teaspoons light brown sugar
¼ cup chopped cilantro

---

1. Heat the oil in the pressure cooker. Add the lamb and season with cumin, salt, and pepper. Cook uncovered over high heat until well browned, about 6 minutes. Pour in the vinegar and stir up any browned bits from the bottom of the pan. Add the potatoes and onion. Sprinkle flour over the surface and mix well. Add beer, chipotle (their heat varies—start by adding ½ of a chile), and brown sugar.
2. Cover and bring up to high pressure. Reduce heat to stabilize pressure and cook 10 minutes. Release pressure and add cilantro.

Moroccan Lamb and Eggplant Stew

The perfume of Middle Eastern spices is often associated with lamb and eggplant. In this stew, they lend a heady aroma and taste. As with so many stews, this one improves if made a day ahead. Try serving it atop plain couscous.

Makes 3 to 4 servings

---

1 tablespoon olive oil
1¼ pounds lamb stew meat, cut in
   1-inch cubes
1 teaspoon ground cumin
½ teaspoon ground oregano
¼ teaspoon cinnamon
⅛ teaspoon cayenne, or more to taste
¼ cup dry red wine
1 tablespoon sherry vinegar or red
   wine vinegar
⅓ cup Beef Stock (page 26) or
   canned broth

3 tablespoons tomato paste
1 tablespoon light brown sugar
2 cups peeled, diced eggplant, cut in
   1-inch cubes
3 tablespoons dried currants
1½ tablespoons chopped fresh mint
1½ tablespoons chopped fresh cilantro
   or parsley
Salt

---

1. Heat the oil in the pressure cooker over high heat. Add the lamb and season with cumin, oregano, cinnamon, and cayenne. Cook uncovered, turning until well browned, 6 to 8 minutes. Pour the wine and vinegar into cooker, then add the stock or broth, tomato paste, and brown sugar.

2. Cover and bring up to high pressure. Reduce heat to stabilize pressure and cook 12 minutes. Release pressure by running cold water over the cover.

3. Add the eggplant and currants. Cover again and return to high pressure. Cook 2 minutes. Release pressure. Add mint and cilantro and season with salt to taste.

Veal Stew with Tangerine and Cumin

Makes 4 servings

1½ pounds lean veal stew meat, cut in 1-inch cubes

2 tablespoons fresh tangerine or orange juice

1 serrano or jalapeño pepper, seeded and minced

2 teaspoons minced fresh ginger

1 shallot, minced

½ teaspoon grated tangerine or orange zest

2 tablespoons vegetable oil

2 tablespoons all-purpose flour

1½ cups peeled, cubed acorn or butternut squash, cut in 1-inch cubes

1 cup canned or fresh peeled, seeded, and diced tomatoes, well drained

½ cup Chicken Stock (page 25) or canned broth

½ teaspoon ground cumin

Salt and freshly ground pepper

---

1. Combine the veal, tangerine juice, hot pepper, ginger, shallot, and tangerine zest in a mixing bowl; toss to combine. Cover and refrigerate 30 minutes.

2. Heat half of the oil in the pressure cooker over medium-high heat. Add half of the veal and cook, turning, until brown, 5 to 7 minutes, set aside. Heat remaining oil and brown the rest of the veal. Return all the meat to the cooker. Sprinkle flour over meat and stir in. Add squash, tomatoes, stock or broth, and cumin.

3. Cover and bring up to high pressure. Reduce heat to stabilize pressure and cook 8 minutes. Release pressure. Season with salt and pepper to taste.

Baked Eggs with Onions and Bacon

This breakfast or brunch custard with its delicate texture is richly flavored with bronze-cooked onions and bacon.

Makes 6 servings

---

2 strips of smoked bacon, diced
4 small onions, sliced
Pinch of dried thyme
½ teaspoon salt
⅛ teaspoon freshly ground pepper
6 large eggs

1 cup whipping cream
¼ cup whole milk
½ teaspoon Dijon mustard
1 tablespoon minced fresh chives, if
    available

---

1. Cook the bacon in a medium skillet or the pressure cooker uncovered over medium heat until it is browned, about 5 minutes. Add the onions, thyme, salt, and pepper, reduce heat to low, and cook until onions are limp and golden, 15 minutes.

2. Whisk eggs; beat in cream, milk, mustard, salt, and pepper and mix thoroughly. Transfer to a 7- to 8-cup casserole that fits easily inside the pressure cooker. Sprinkle chives over top, if using. Cover casserole with foil, fitting it closely so no water can get inside.

3. Put the steamer insert in the pressure cooker and add 2 cups of water. Carefully add casserole. Cover pressure cooker and bring up to high pressure. Reduce heat to stabilize pressure and cook 23 minutes. Release pressure by running cold water over the lid. Remove foil and let stand 10 minutes before serving.

Pasta and Pasta Sauces

Have you had enough pasta? Not if you're like most Americans. Consumption of this complex carbohydrate has skyrocketed, turning into a healthy obsession. We have wisely caught on to the fact that pasta needn't be fattening, and a wonderful world of possibilities beyond spaghetti and macaroni is open for us to explore. Fusilli, penne, rotelle, tortellini, and linguine are becoming dinner staples, and the range of sauces that tops them has expanded to infinite variety.

Because the trend clearly shows we're consuming more pasta than ever before, I wanted to offer as complete a range of pressure cooker recipes as possible. This means lots of luscious sauces. Here you'll find traditional pasta sauces, such as marinara, the classic red sauce of Naples; puttanesca, a simple sauce with a "big" taste; and Bolognese sauce, one of the most revered sauces in Italian cookery. Each of these sauces suggests uses beyond pasta. Marinara mixes with eggplant or tops goat cheese. It can add élan to poached chicken or grilled fish, and it elevates steamed mussels to star status. Bolognese ragu or veal ragu can be spooned over soft polenta or rice, while strips of turkey or chicken turn puttanesca sauce into a simple sauté.

Packages of fresh pastas shapes, a fairly recent entry into the refrigerator cases of most supermarkets, and several of the tiniest dried shapes, are ideally suited to the pressure cooker. Combined with simple sauce ingredients, the two cook together in tandem in minutes—without boiling a separate pot of water.

Hints and tips:
- In recipes where pasta and sauce are cooked together, be sure to use the varieties and sizes specified.
- Fresh angel hair, linguine, and fettuccine do not cook acceptably in the pressure cooker.
- Tiny dried shells, orzo, and pastina can be cooked and sauced together in the pressure cooker. Other shapes do not cook properly.
- Do not double those recipes in which pasta and sauce cook together; the pressure cooker will be too crowded for them to cook properly.
- If you're not using your pressure cooker to make the sauce, it doubles as a pasta cooker when it is used without the cover.

Veal Ragu

Italian ragus—thick pasta sauces—are quite different from what they are often perceived to be. Tiny cubes of meat are simmered with bits of vegetables, meat broth, and aromatic herbs. A small amount of cream often adds a smooth, rounded taste. This classic is particularly good over tagliatelle or fettuccine.

Makes 4 to 6 servings

---

3 tablespoons olive oil
1 small onion, chopped
1 medium carrot, finely diced
1 medium celery rib, finely diced
¼ teaspoon dried rosemary, crushed
¼ teaspoon dried basil
1 pound veal shoulder, cut in ¼-inch
    cubes

¼ cup dry white wine
⅔ cup Chicken Stock (page 25) or
    canned broth
1 tablespoon tomato paste
¼ cup whipping cream
2 medium tomatoes, seeded and finely
    chopped
Salt and freshly ground pepper

---

1. Heat the oil in the pressure cooker over medium-high heat. Add the onion, carrot, celery, rosemary, and basil. Cook uncovered until onion begins to soften, 3 to 4 minutes. Add the veal and cook, stirring occasionally, until it is no longer pink, 3 to 5 minutes. Add wine and cook 1 minute. Add stock or broth and tomato paste.

2. Cover and bring up to high pressure. Reduce heat to stabilize pressure and cook 7 minutes. Release pressure and add cream. Boil uncovered until mixture thickens, 4 to 5 minutes. Add tomatoes and season with salt and pepper to taste. Cook 1 to 2 minutes to heat through.

Bolognese Ragu

The similarities between a classic Bolognese sauce and this extra-speedy version are remarkable. The biggest difference is that several hours are sheared off. For the best results, avoid using beef ground for hamburgers; it is too fine. Either dice it yourself or ask for coarsely ground or for chili grind.

Makes 6 servings

---

4 ounces salt pork, finely diced
2 large carrots, very finely diced
1 large celery rib, very finely diced
1 small onion, very finely diced
1 pound boneless beef chuck blade,
  very finely diced or coarsely ground

½ cup whipping cream
¼ cup dry vermouth
2 tablespoons tomato paste
1 teaspoon chopped fresh rosemary or
  ½ teaspoon dried
Salt and freshly ground pepper

---

1. Cook the salt pork in the pressure cooker uncovered over medium heat until most of the fat is rendered, 8 to 10 minutes. Add carrots, celery, and onion and cook 1 minute. Add the beef and cook, stirring until lightly browned, about 4 minutes. Add cream, vermouth, tomato paste, and rosemary.

2. Cover and bring up to high pressure. Reduce heat to stabilize pressure and cook 5 minutes. Release pressure. Season with salt and pepper to taste.

Spicy Marinara Sauce

The summery taste of fresh, vine-ripened tomatoes is captured in this sauce that has a thousand uses. Be sure to use plump rosy tomatoes that have ripened on the vine.

Makes 3 cups

---

3 tablespoons olive oil
1 small red onion, chopped
1 small carrot, finely diced
2 large garlic cloves, minced
2 small dried red chiles
¼ cup dry red wine

2¼ pounds tomatoes, peeled, seeded, and chopped
2 tablespoons tomato paste
3 tablespoons minced fresh basil
Salt and freshly ground pepper

---

1. Heat the oil in the pressure cooker over medium heat. Add the onion, carrot, garlic, and dried chiles. Cook uncovered, stirring often, until vegetables begin to soften, about 4 minutes. Add the wine, increase heat to high, and cook 1 minute. Add tomatoes.

2. Cover and bring up to high pressure. Reduce heat to stabilize pressure and cook 8 minutes. Release pressure and add tomato paste. Boil uncovered 4 to 5 minutes to thicken. Remove dried red chiles, add basil, and season with salt and pepper to taste.

Sausage, Sweet Pepper, and Tomato Sauce

Simple and colorful, this sauce can be used atop polenta as well as over pasta.

Makes 3 cups

½ pound Italian sausage, removed
  from casing
1 small onion, chopped
1 small red bell pepper, cut in ¾-inch
  dice
1 small yellow bell pepper, cut in
  ¾-inch dice

1 can (28 ounces) plum tomatoes,
  drained and diced
1 tablespoon tomato paste
Dash of crushed hot pepper flakes
3 tablespoons whipping cream
Salt and freshly ground pepper

1. Crumble the sausage in the pressure cooker and cook uncovered over medium heat until it begins to brown, about 5 minutes. Add the onion and bell peppers. Increase heat to high and cook until peppers begin to soften, 3 to 4 minutes. Add the tomatoes, tomato paste, and hot pepper flakes.

2. Cover and bring up to high pressure. Reduce heat to stabilize pressure and cook 4 minutes. Release pressure and add cream. Boil uncovered until slightly thickened, 4 to 5 minutes. Season with salt and pepper to taste.

Mushroom and Tomato Pasta Sauce

Flavor abounds in this colorful topping for pasta. Tubular shaped pasta such as penne is ideal for serving.

Makes 4 servings

¼ ounce dried mushrooms, such as cepes or porcini

3 tablespoons olive oil

2 ounces prosciutto, diced

1 large shallot, minced

1 garlic clove, minced

½ teaspoon dried rosemary

1 pound mushrooms, halved or quartered if large

⅔ cup dry white wine

2 medium tomatoes, diced

2 tablespoons whipped cream

Salt and freshly ground pepper

Grated Parmesan cheese, for serving

---

1. Put the dried mushrooms in a small dish and cover with ¼ cup hot water; let stand 20 minutes. Remove and chop mushrooms. Strain liquid and set aside.

2. Heat the oil in the pressure cooker. Add the prosciutto, shallot, garlic, and rosemary. Cook uncovered over medium-high heat, stirring often, until fragrant, 2 to 3 minutes. Add dried and fresh mushrooms; cook 1 minute. Add the mushroom soaking liquid, wine, and half of the diced tomatoes.

3. Cover and bring up to high pressure. Reduce heat to stabilize pressure and cook 5 minutes. Release pressure. Add remaining tomato and the cream. Boil, uncovered, for 3 to 4 minutes. Season with salt and pepper to taste. Pass Parmesan cheese on the side.

Puttanesca Sauce

Puttanesca is a lusty classic Italian sauce, full of zesty flavor and exceptionally quick to prepare.

Makes 3 cups

---

3 tablespoons olive oil
3 large garlic cloves, chopped
4 flat anchovy fillets
1 teaspoon dried sage
¼ to ½ teaspoon crushed hot pepper
   flakes
2 cans (16 ounces each) diced
   tomatoes

3 tablespoons tomato paste
2 tablespoons drained capers
¼ cup chopped black olives, preferably
   oil-cured
¼ cup grated Romano cheese, plus additional cheese for serving
3 tablespoons chopped fresh parsley
Salt and freshly ground black pepper

---

1. Heat the oil in the pressure cooker over low heat. Add the garlic, anchovies, sage, and hot pepper flakes. Cook, stirring often, until garlic is soft but not brown, about 5 minutes. As the mixture cooks, use the back of a wooden spoon to mash the anchovies into a paste.

2. Drain only 1 can of the tomatoes. Add both cans of tomatoes and the liquid from 1 can to the cooker. Add the tomato paste, capers, and olives.

3. Cover and bring up to high pressure. Reduce heat to stabilize pressure and cook 7 minutes. Release pressure and mix in cheese, parsley, and salt and pepper to taste.

Ravioli with Gorgonzola and Sage Cream

Sauce and pasta cook together in one step in about 10 minutes. Be sure to use fresh ravioli; dried will not cook properly.

Makes 2 to 3 servings

1 package (9 ounces) fresh cheese- or meat-filled ravioli
1 cup Chicken Stock (page 25) or canned broth, or Vegetable Stock (page 24)
1 small garlic clove, minced

1 teaspoon rubbed sage
¼ cup whipping cream
¼ cup crumbled Gorgonzola cheese
2 tablespoons grated Parmesan cheese, plus additional for serving
Salt and freshly ground pepper

1. Combine the ravioli, stock or broth, garlic, and sage in the pressure cooker. Cover and bring up to high pressure. Reduce heat to stabilize pressure and cook 2 minutes. Release pressure.

2. Return the cooker to high heat. Add cream and boil uncovered until the mixture thickens slightly, about 2 minutes. Reduce heat to medium and add the Gorgonzola and Parmesan cheese. Cook, stirring, until sauce is smooth, 1 to 2 minutes. Season with salt and pepper to taste. Serve with a sprinkling of additional grated Parmesan cheese on top.

Spicy Shells with Broccoli

As quick as heating up a frozen dinner or boiling a pot of water, this simple pasta dish is ideal for a light after-work dinner. Be sure the shells are the size specified. If you are making this for children, feel free to omit the hot pepper flakes.

Makes 2 to 4 servings

1¼ cups Chicken Stock (page 25) or canned broth, or Vegetable Stock (page 24)
¾ cup small (½-inch) shell pasta
1 large garlic clove, minced

¼ teaspoon crushed hot pepper flakes
1 small stalk broccoli, finely chopped
1 tablespoon unsalted butter
Salt and freshly ground pepper
Grated Parmesan cheese, for serving

1. Combine the stock or broth, pasta, garlic, and hot pepper flakes in the pressure cooker. Cover and bring up to high pressure. Reduce heat to stabilize pressure and cook 3 minutes. Release pressure and add the broccoli. Cover and return to high pressure. Remove from heat as soon as high pressure is reached.

2. Add the butter and cook uncovered over high heat, tossing, for 1 to 2 minutes, until the liquid thickens to a saucy consistency. Season with salt and pepper to taste and pass grated Parmesan cheese on the side.

Tortellini with Prosciutto and Peas

Fast, easy, and fresh—three important assets for after-work dinners. Be sure to use fresh tortellini from the refrigerator case. Dried pasta will not cook properly.

Makes 2 servings

1 package (9 ounces) fresh meat- or
   cheese-filled tortellini
1 cup Chicken Stock (page 25) or
   canned broth
1 small garlic clove, minced
½ teaspoon dried basil
⅓ cup tiny frozen peas, thawed

¼ cup whipping cream
¼ cup finely grated Parmesan cheese,
   plus additional cheese for serving
2 ounces prosciutto, diced
1 scallion, sliced
Salt and freshly ground pepper

1. Combine the tortellini, stock or broth, garlic, and basil in the pressure cooker. Cover and bring up to high pressure. Reduce heat to stabilize pressure and cook 2 minutes.

2. Release pressure and add peas, cream, ¼ cup cheese, prosciutto, and scallion. Boil uncovered over high heat until slightly thickened, about 1 minute. Season with salt and pepper to taste and serve with additional cheese on the side.

Beans and Lentils

If only one food had to justify the entire cost of a pressure cooker, dried beans would make the purchase more than worthwhile. While duly impressive claims, such as "three times quicker," apply to many foods prepared under pressure, dried beans exceed that many times over. When the pressure cooker is called upon, all varieties of soaked beans are ready in less than 15 minutes. Compare that to times that often exceed 2 hours when the beans are cooked by the conventional method, and it becomes even more remarkable.

The saga of dried beans is a story of rags to riches and social climbing. Once barely noticed in the American diet, except occasionally as the substance of baked beans or the support in a bowl of chili, they have now earned mainstream approval. Rich in protein and fiber, and inexpensive, they are also very low in fat and free of cholesterol. Bland in their own right, they become lively and flavorful when allowed to associate with the right ingredients. Garlic, herbs, tomatoes, sausage, and rich stocks all have the capacity to turn a humble pot of beans into a fine feast. Further moving them up the ladder of success is their prominence in French bistro and Italian trattoria cooking.

Most supermarkets carry six to eight varieties of dried beans, among them kidney, black, pinto, black-eyes, navy, limas, Great

Northern, and garbanzo beans (also called chick-peas). Increasingly, "boutique" beans are showing up in specialty markets: unusually colored calypso, rattlesnake, soldier, Anasazi, and Maine, or Steuben, yellow-eyes are among these offerings. By all means, add them to your repertoire if you come across them. Cooking times can be estimated for these types by comparing them to familiar beans of similar size and shape.

Lentils are similarly quick and successful in the pressure cooker. And since they don't require soaking before cooking, they practically fall into the convenience food category.

Hints and tips:
- Soaked and drained beans can be refrigerated for 2 days before cooking, or frozen for up to 2 months.
- Beans and lentils foam as they cook, so the cooker should never be filled more than halfway.
- There may be some sputtering as the cooker depressurizes. If it's convenient, I transfer the cooker to the sink to prevent spills.
- Running cold water over the cover stops the cooking more quickly and minimizes sputtering.
- Always check the valve after cooking beans or lentils to make sure a loosened skin isn't clogging it.

Basic Cooked Beans

Here are guidelines for cooking many varieties of dried beans. Though technically soaking beans overnight isn't necessary, I highly recommend doing so. It rinses away some of the complex sugars that make beans difficult for many people to digest, and it also makes cooking quicker and more reliable. The alternative quick-soak method does just fine in a pinch. As a rule of thumb, dried beans double after soaking and cooking; 1 cup of dried beans will measure about 2 cups after rehydrating, with a little difference between varieties.

The California Dried Bean Association advises that adding salt to the soaking water improves the ability of beans to absorb water. Most sources advise against adding salt to the cooking water, claiming it makes the skin tough. However, recent research refutes the practice, noting that the amount of salt used to flavor beans has no effect on the skin. In light of this, I do add some salt to the cooking water. It is strictly optional, though. Flavorings such as garlic, onions, and herbs can be added to the cooking water as desired. Drained soaked beans can be refrigerated for 2 days or frozen up to 2 months before cooking.

Makes 4 to 6 servings

1½ cups dried beans   Salt

---

1. Put beans in a large bowl and add 4 cups water and 1 teaspoon salt. Let stand 12 hours or overnight. For quick soaking, put beans, 4 cups water, and 1 teaspoon salt in the pressure cooker. Cover and bring up to high pressure. Remove from heat and release pressure by running cold water over the cover. Let stand for 3 hours.

(continued on next page)

2. Drain and rinse the beans and transfer to the pressure cooker. Add 5 cups fresh water and 1 teaspoon salt. Cover and bring up to high pressure. Reduce heat to stabilize pressure and cook for the times indicated below. Release pressure by running cold water over the cover. If your cooker has a pressure release valve on the handle, do not open it until all the pressure has been released; this minimizes foaming. Drain beans.

NOTE: Cooking times of beans are variable. Age, the season they were harvested, and where they were grown all play a part. However, the times given below are good estimates for beans that are tender but still hold their shape. If you like softer beans or want to puree them, increase cooking time by 50 percent to 100 percent.

Adzuki	5 to 7 minutes
Anasazi	4 to 6 minutes
Appaloosa	9 to 11 minutes
Black beans	7 to 9 minutes
Black-eyed peas	3 to 4 minutes
Calypso	4 to 6 minutes
Chick-peas (garbanzos)	10 to 12 minutes
Cranberry	8 to 10 minutes
Flageolets	10 to 12 minutes
Great Northern	7 to 9 minutes
Kidney	7 to 9 minutes
Lima beans	3 to 5 minutes
Pigeon peas	5 to 7 minutes
Pintos	5 to 7 minutes
Navy pea	3 to 5 minutes
Red	4 to 6 minutes
Scarlet runner	10 to 12 minutes
Snow cap	10 to 12 minutes
Soy	10 to 12 minutes
Yellow-eye	10 to 12 minutes

Beans with Tomatoes and Peppery Ham Broth

Subtle smoky undertones, a blast of black pepper, and ripe tomatoes enliven a humble bean recipe.

Makes 4 to 6 servings

---

8 ounces Great Northern beans, soaked overnight

1¾ cups Ham Stock (page 27)

¾ teaspoon coarsely ground pepper

1 teaspoon light brown sugar

2 large ripe tomatoes, seeded and diced

2 teaspoons chopped fresh sage or 1 teaspoon dried

1 teaspoon balsamic vinegar

Salt and freshly ground pepper

---

1. Combine the drained beans, ham stock, pepper, and brown sugar in the pressure cooker. Cover and bring up to high pressure. Reduce heat to stabilize pressure and cook 8 minutes. Release pressure by running cold water over the cover.

2. Toss beans with tomatoes, sage, and vinegar. Season with salt and pepper to taste. Serve warm or at room temperature.

Ponderosa Pintos

Your favorite recipe for Boston baked beans may become part of the past, traded in for classic cowboy beans. They go alongside brisket as easily as grilled bratwurst.

Makes 6 to 8 servings

---

2 cups pinto beans, soaked overnight
6 cups water
6 ounces smoked slab bacon, finely
   diced
1 medium onion, chopped
1½ teaspoons chili powder

⅛ to ¼ teaspoon cayenne
1 cup beer
2 large tomatoes, diced
⅔ cup prepared barbecue sauce
Salt and coarsely ground black pepper

---

1. Combine the drained beans and 6 cups fresh water in the pressure cooker. Cover and bring up to high pressure. Reduce heat to stabilize pressure and cook 8 minutes. Release pressure by running cold water over the cover. Drain beans and set aside.
2. Brown the bacon with the onion, chili powder, and cayenne in the pressure cooker over medium-low heat. Add beer and stir up the browned bits from the bottom of the pan. Heat to a boil and cook 1 minute. Add drained beans, tomatoes, and barbecue sauce.
3. Cover and bring up to high pressure. Cook 2 minutes. Release pressure. Season with salt and a generous amount of black pepper to taste.

Smokin' Red Beans and Rice

Chipotles are smoked jalapeño peppers. Here one is used not only to add a spicy hot kick, but also to add the smoky taste more typically coaxed from a big ham bone or ham hocks. It's a clever trick for many rice and bean dishes; it cuts down on fat and appeals to vegetarians.

Makes 6 to 8 servings

¾ cup red beans, soaked overnight
3 tablespoons vegetable oil
2 large garlic cloves, minced
3 celery ribs, sliced
1 large green bell pepper, diced
1 cup converted white rice
1 can (16 ounces) diced tomatoes
1¾ cups Chicken Stock ((page 25) or
    canned broth, or Vegetable Stock
    (page 24)

1 teaspoon dried thyme
1 dried chipotle chile, soaked to soften
    and minced
Salt and Tabasco sauce, to taste
4 large scallions, sliced
½ cup chopped fresh cilantro or
    parsley

---

1. Heat the oil in the pressure cooker. Add the garlic, celery, and bell pepper. Cook over medium-high heat until vegetables begin to soften, 3 to 4 minutes. Add the rice, drained beans, tomatoes with their liquid, stock or broth, thyme, and chipotle chile.

2. Cover and bring up to high pressure. Reduce heat to stabilize pressure and cook 10 minutes. Release pressure and add salt, Tabasco, scallions, and cilantro.

Spicy Black-Eyes and Beans with Rice

Legend has it that black-eye peas bring good luck. Who's to say if it's true or not, but it's worth the bet. Inky color leaches from black beans when they're soaked, so soak the peas and beans separately.

Makes 4 to 6 servings

⅓ cup black-eyed peas, soaked overnight

⅓ cup black beans, soaked overnight

8 to 10 ounces andouille sausage, diced

1 small onion, chopped

2 celery ribs, chopped

1 teaspoon dried thyme

⅔ cup converted white rice

1 can (10 ounces) diced tomatoes with chiles

2½ cups water or Vegetable Stock (page 24)

Salt and freshly ground pepper

Chopped fresh cilantro

---

1. Put the sausage in the pressure cooker and cook over medium heat until it begins to brown and render some fat. Add the onion, celery, and thyme. Cook uncovered until onion begins to soften, about 4 minutes. Add the drained peas and beans, the rice, tomatoes with their liquid, and water or vegetable stock.

2. Cover and bring up to high pressure. Reduce heat to stabilize pressure and cook 12 minutes. Release pressure by running cold water over the cover. Season with salt and pepper to taste and sprinkle with chopped cilantro.

Mussels with Saffron Cream

The affinity of mussels with saffron is a story of rags and riches. Mussels are among the least expensive of the sea's treasures, while saffron can cost a king's ransom. But just a pinch is used in a worthy indulgence.

Makes 2 to 3 servings

---

1 tablespoon unsalted butter
2 large shallots, minced
1 medium carrot, finely diced
½ of a small red bell pepper, finely diced
¾ cup dry white wine

⅛ teaspoon saffron threads
2 pounds mussels, scrubbed and debearded
⅓ cup whipping cream
3 tablespoons chopped fresh basil
Freshly ground pepper

---

1. Melt the butter in the pressure cooker. Add the shallots, carrot, and bell pepper. Cook uncovered over medium heat until carrot is soft, about 5 minutes. Add the wine and saffron. Heat to a boil. Add mussels.

2. Cover and bring up to high pressure over high heat. As soon as high pressure is reached, remove from heat. Release pressure by running cold water over the lid.

3. Divide mussels among serving bowls. Boil the liquid in the pan 3 minutes to reduce. Add cream, basil, and any accumulated juices from mussels. Boil until cream thickens slightly, 4 to 5 minutes. Season with pepper to taste and pour over mussels.

Whitefish en Papillote

En papillote *is a classic cooking method of cooking meat, fish, poultry, or vegetables in sealed paper packets. While they are often baked in a very hot oven, they are sometimes steamed. The preparation adapts beautifully to the pressure cooker. Sea bass can be used in place of whitefish. Just be sure the fillets aren't too thick, or they won't cook properly.*

Makes 2 servings

---

3 tablespoons dry white wine or dry vermouth
2 tablespoons olive oil
2 small plum tomatoes, sliced
1 medium shallot, sliced
½ cup diced marinated artichoke hearts

¼ teaspoon salt
⅛ teaspoon freshly ground pepper
2 tablespoons minced fresh parsley
1 tablespoon minced fresh tarragon or ¾ teaspoon dried
2 whitefish fillets (about 6 ounces each), cut ½ inch thick

---

1. Combine the wine and olive oil; set aside. Fold in half 2 sheets of parchment paper about 15 inches square; open flat on counter. Arrange overlapping slices of tomato just above the fold on each sheet. Scatter the shallot slices and artichokes over the tomatoes. Season with half the salt and pepper and drizzle lightly with wine-oil mixture. Sprinkle half of the herbs over the vegetables. Top each with a fish fillet, season with the remaining salt and pepper, and add the remaining oil mixture and herbs.

2. Fold and crimp the packets to form half-moons. Seal the edges so they are airtight; use paper clips, if necessary.

---

3. Put the steamer insert in pressure cooker and add 1½ cups water. Place the packets on the steamer insert. Cover and bring up to high pressure. Reduce heat to stabilize pressure and cook 6 minutes. Release pressure by running cold water over the lid. Transfer the packets to serving plates.

Salmon with Creamy Cabbage and Leeks

Cabbage, sometimes thought of as a plebeian vegetable, rises to star status in this elegant preparation. Smoky bacon, bits of leeks, and a little mustard make it well suited to serving with fresh salmon.

Makes 2 servings

---

1 tablespoon vegetable oil
1 slice of bacon, finely diced
1 small leek, finely diced
12 ounces Savoy or green cabbage, cut in thin ribbons
½ cup Chicken Stock (page 25) or canned broth
¼ cup dry white wine

1 teaspoon grainy Dijon mustard
1 teaspoon dried thyme
½ of a small red bell pepper, very finely diced
2 tablespoons sour cream
Salt and freshly ground pepper
2 salmon fillets, about 6 ounces each

---

1. Heat the oil in the pressure cooker over medium heat. Add the bacon and leek. Cook uncovered, stirring often, until the bacon is well browned, 3 to 5 minutes. Add the cabbage, stock or broth, wine, mustard, and thyme.

2. Cover and bring up to full pressure. Reduce heat to stabilize pressure and cook for 2 minutes. Release pressure by running cold water over cover.

3. Stir the bell pepper, sour cream, ¼ teaspoon salt, and ⅛ teaspoon pepper into cabbage. Place the salmon fillets on top, placing them skin side down. Cover the pressure cooker. Start timing immediately and cook exactly 4 minutes. Release pressure by running cold water over the cover. Season the fish lightly with additional salt and pepper.

Sicilian Swordfish with Minted Tomato Sauce

The addition of a handful of fresh mint distinguishes this southern Italian recipe, adding a clean refreshing finish. Fresh tuna or mahimahi can also be used.

Makes 2 servings

3 tablespoons olive oil
1 large garlic clove, thinly sliced
Pinch of crushed hot pepper flakes
¼ teaspoon salt
½ of a small onion, chopped
½ cup finely diced fresh fennel bulb

1 cup finely diced tomatoes, fresh or
  canned
¼ cup dry white wine
¼ cup fresh mint leaves, chopped
2 swordfish steaks (about 5 ounces
  each), cut ½ inch thick

1. Heat the oil, garlic, hot pepper, and salt in the pressure cooker over medium-high heat. When the garlic begins to color, remove it with a slotted spoon and discard. Add the onion and fennel. Cook uncovered until the fennel begins to soften, 2 minutes. Add tomatoes, wine, and about ⅔ of the mint. Simmer 1 minute. Place fish on top; season lightly with salt and add remaining mint.

2. Cover and bring up to high pressure. Reduce heat to stabilize pressure and cook exactly 2½ minutes. Release pressure by running cold water over the cover. Serve at once.

Tuna Steaks with Sweet/Sour Onion Relish

Grilling fish is the cooking method of choice for many cooks. The pressure cooker should be considered a close second. It does the job quickly and without a lot of fuss. Here a savory onion relish cooks at the same time and in the same pan.

Makes 2 servings

1½ teaspoons Dijon mustard
⅓ cup orange juice
¼ teaspoon dried tarragon
Salt and cayenne
2 tuna steaks (5 to 6 ounces each),
  cut ½ inch thick
1½ tablespoons unsalted butter

1 medium onion, cut in ½-inch
  wedges
1 small red bell pepper, cut in 2 by
  ½-inch strips
1½ tablespoons balsamic vinegar
½ teaspoon honey
⅓ cup dry white wine

---

1. Combine the mustard, 1 tablespoon orange juice, and a pinch each of tarragon, salt, and cayenne. Brush on fish and let stand for 20 minutes.
2. Melt 1 tablespoon butter in the pressure cooker over medium-high heat. Add the onion and bell pepper. Cook uncovered, stirring often, until the onion begins to brown at the edges, 3 to 4 minutes. Add the vinegar and honey; cook 30 seconds. Add the remaining orange juice and tarragon, and the wine. Place fish on top and season lightly with salt and cayenne.
3. Cover and bring up to high pressure. Reduce heat to stabilize pressure and cook 2½ minutes for a slightly pink center, 3 minutes for fully cooked tuna. Release pressure by running cold water over the cover.
4. Set tuna aside and keep warm. Boil onion mixture in cooker over high heat to thicken slightly, about 1 minute. Stir in the remaining butter and serve.

Fish and Seafood

Swordfish with Basque Tomato Sauce

A simple and colorful way to present swordfish. As in all methods of fish cookery, timing is critical. Add more time as necessary but take care not to overcook.

Makes 4 servings

1½ tablespoons olive oil
1 garlic clove, minced
1 medium onion, cut in thin wedges
¼ teaspoon dried thyme
Salt and freshly ground pepper
1 tablespoon sherry wine vinegar
3 medium tomatoes, cut in 1-inch dice
1 small roasted red bell pepper, cut in
    1-inch squares

1 tablespoon tomato paste
Pinch of sugar
⅓ cup dry white wine
4 swordfish steaks (about 5 ounces
    each), cut ½ inch thick
8 lemon slices
2 tablespoons minced parsley

---

1. Heat the oil in the pressure cooker over medium-high heat. Add the garlic, onion, thyme, and a dash of salt and pepper. Cook uncovered, stirring often, until onion begins to brown at the edges, 3 to 5 minutes. Add vinegar. When it stops sizzling, add the tomatoes, bell pepper, tomato paste, and sugar. Cook until heated through, 1 minute. Add the wine. Arrange the swordfish on top and season fish lightly with salt and pepper. Top each steak with 2 slices of lemon.
2. Cover and bring up to high pressure. Reduce heat to stabilize pressure and cook exactly 3 minutes. Release pressure by running cold water over the cover. The fish should be cooked through. If it is not, place cover on and let stand 3 to 4 minutes. Serve the fish topped with tomato sauce and minced parsley.

Stews and One-Dish Meals

Stews are among the most evocative of all foods. The word alone can call to mind fond memories of Sunday supper, of grandmother's house, of life's simple pleasures, which so often can be found around the dinner table. Add the haunting aroma as they cook, the rich flavors, and the sustaining comfort so generously proffered, and it's small wonder that stews continue to be popular all across America.

The pressure cooker does nothing to change the homey script that generations of cooks have so carefully recorded through the stewpot. All it does is cook these marvelous dishes more quickly, an adjustment that's hard for anyone to object to. A two-hour stew can come to the table in about a quarter of the time, chili in five minutes, and jambalaya and gumbos in ten. And almost every dish of this type reheats well, adding an extra element of ease to a cook's agenda.

The convenience of dishes that combine meat, starchy food-stuffs, and vegetables in one course is widely appealing. The same strategy also fits nicely into the health-minded trend toward less meat and more vegetables and complex carbohydrates. Cooks have a large amount of control over what they add to stews: If a greater ratio of vegetables to meat suits your style, most recipes of this type easily accommodate such changes. And, in recipes where the meat

is browned in oil as a preliminary step, those who are on a low-fat diet can eliminate this step and reduce fat even more.

Hints and tips:
- When browning meat in the pressure cooker, don't overcrowd it. Cook in batches as necessary, depending on the size of your cooker.
- In many recipes, vegetables are added toward the end of cooking, so they stay vibrant, fresh, and crisp-tender. As you adapt your own recipes for the pressure cooker, use the same strategy.
- When making your own recipes in the pressure cooker, you may have to adjust the amount of liquid. Since there is very little evaporation, many recipes require less liquid in the pressure cooker than you may be used to in a standard Dutch oven or casserole. Just be sure to add the minimum amount recommended in your user's manual.
- As the capacity of your cooker allows, consider making double recipes and freezing the extra.
- Pressure cookers are great for tailgating and potlucks. Once the food is cooked, leave the cooker covered and locked and let the pressure release naturally. The food stays hot inside for several hours.

Chicken and Sausage Gumbo

The pressure cooker does a marvelous job of quickly coaxing flavor and character into a pot of gumbo. Alas, it does not offer a solution to making roux the traditional way, and that must be done first, uncovered. Roux thickens gumbo, imparting mouth-filling richness, so mastering it is essential. Once it is done, the rest is easy. If your pressure cooker is made of lightweight aluminum, you'll have better results making the roux in a heavy skillet or saucepan and transferring it to the cooker.

Makes 6 servings

¼ cup vegetable oil

¼ cup all-purpose flour

2 small bell peppers, preferably 1 red and 1 green, diced

3 small celery ribs, diced

1 medium onion, diced

2 garlic cloves, minced

4 cups Chicken Stock (page 25) or canned broth

2 tablespoons Cajun seasoning blend

1 teaspoon Tabasco sauce

½ pound okra, cut in ½-inch-thick slices

½ pound andouille sausage, cut in ½-inch-thick slices

2 cups cooked chicken (about ½ pound), torn into large pieces

Salt and freshly ground pepper

---

1. To make the roux, heat the oil in the pressure cooker or a heavy pan until it is very hot. Gradually mix in the flour. Cook over medium-high heat, stirring constantly, until the mixture is a rich medium brown, 4 to 5 minutes. Watch carefully so it does not burn. Quickly but carefully—the roux is very hot!—add the bell peppers, celery, and onion. Reduce the heat to medium. Cook 1 minute, stirring constantly. Add the garlic and then the stock or broth, seasoning blend, Tabasco sauce, and okra.

2. If you have used another pan, transfer the mixture to the pressure cooker. Cover and bring up to high pressure. Reduce the heat to stabilize pressure and cook 5 minutes. Release pressure and add the sausage, chicken, and salt and pepper to taste.

Gumbo Z'Herbes

The myriad influences that characterize Creole cooking are deliciously evident in this thick and potent gumbo. African, French, Acadian, and the cooking of the American South all play a hand here.

Makes 6 servings

⅓ cup vegetable oil

⅓ cup all-purpose flour

1 medium onion, diced

1 green bell pepper, diced

2 celery ribs, sliced

1 small bunch of red Swiss chard, stems sliced, leaves chopped

2 garlic cloves, minced

½ pound andouille or spicy smoked sausage, sliced

2 cups cooked chicken, turkey, or duck (about ½ pound), pulled into large shreds

3½ cups Chicken Stock (page 25) or canned broth

1 tablespoon Creole seasoning blend

5 ounces fresh spinach, coarsely chopped

5 ounces mixed greens, such as mustard, turnip, or tender collards, coarsely chopped

Salt and cayenne

1. Heat the oil in the pressure cooker until it is almost smoking. (If you have a lightweight aluminum pressure cooker, make the roux in a heavy saucepan and transfer it to the pressure cooker.) Add the flour, stirring until smooth. Cook over medium-high heat, stirring constantly, until the roux takes on a rich medium-brown color, 4 to 5 minutes.

2. As soon as the right color is reached, carefully add the onion, bell pepper, celery, and stems of the chard. Cook, stirring often, for 3 minutes. Add the garlic, sausage, and poultry; cook 1 minute. Slowly add the stock or broth, then stir in the Creole seasoning. Add the Swiss chard leaves, spinach, and greens, stirring them into the broth.

3. Cover and bring up to high pressure. Reduce heat to stabilize pressure and cook 5 minutes. Release pressure. Season with salt and cayenne to taste and serve.

Hunter-style Chicken and Sausage Stew

Chicken cacciatore has inspired this recipe, although the addition of sausage sets it apart from the classic Italian dish. Pasta or polenta can be served alongside to soak up the juices.

Makes 4 servings

---

3 tablespoons olive oil
1 small red bell pepper, cut in 6 wedges
1 small green bell pepper, cut in 6 wedges
4 ounces mushrooms, preferably a brown cap type, halved (or quartered if large)
1 medium onion, cut in wedges
¼ teaspoon salt

⅛ teaspoon freshly ground pepper
1 (3½-pound) chicken, cut in serving pieces
6 ounces Italian-style turkey sausage or Italian sausage in casing, cut in 1-inch pieces
1½ tablespoons red wine vinegar
1 can (16 ounces) diced tomatoes
1 teaspoon dried rosemary
½ teaspoon dried basil

---

1. Heat 2 tablespoons of the oil in the pressure cooker over high heat. Add the bell peppers, mushrooms, onion, and some salt and pepper. Cook uncovered until the vegetables begin to brown at the edges, 4 to 5 minutes. Remove them from the cooker and set aside.

2. Heat the remaining 1 tablespoon oil in cooker over medium-high heat. Add the chicken and sausage and cook, turning, until browned well on both sides, 6 to 8 minutes. Carefully pour off excess oil. Return cooker to medium-high heat. Pour in vinegar. When it has cooked away, add the reserved vegetables, the tomatoes with their liquid, and the rosemary and basil.

3. Cover and bring up to low pressure. Reduce heat to stabilize pressure and cook 16 minutes. Release pressure. Season with additional salt and pepper to taste and serve.

Jambalaya

One-dish meals are a boon to the cook, especially if they proffer taste and style. Jambalaya, the Creole creation of rice, tomatoes, and a variety of meats, sausage, and seafood, has plenty of both, here with the added bonus of cooking in a matter of minutes.

Makes 4 to 6 servings

1 tablespoon vegetable oil
10 ounces skinless, boneless chicken
    breast, cut in ¾-inch-thick strips
½ pound andouille or other spicy
    smoked sausage, sliced
6 ounces peeled, deveined shrimp
    (optional)
2 teaspoons Creole seasoning blend
1 teaspoon dried thyme
⅛ to ¼ teaspoon cayenne to taste

1 medium onion, chopped
1 large green bell pepper, chopped
3 celery ribs, sliced
1 cup converted white rice
1 can (16 ounces) diced tomatoes or
    Creole-style stewed tomatoes
1 cup Chicken Stock (page 25) or
    canned broth
3 tablespoons minced parsley
Salt

1. Heat the oil in the pressure cooker over medium-high heat. Add the chicken, sausage, and shrimp. Season with half of the Creole seasoning, thyme, and cayenne. Cook uncovered, stirring often, until the chicken is white throughout, 3 to 4 minutes. Remove with a slotted spoon and set aside.

2. Add the onion, bell pepper, celery, and remaining Creole seasoning, thyme, and cayenne. Cook, stirring often, until the vegetables begin to soften, 4 to 5 minutes. Add the rice, tomatoes with their liquid, and stock or broth.

3. Cover and bring up to high pressure. Reduce heat to stabilize pressure and cook 8 minutes. Release pressure and add the chicken, sausage, shrimp, and parsley. Cover and let stand for 5 minutes. Season with salt and more cayenne to taste.

Chaco Chicken Chili

Howlin' hot and deliciously spiced, this chili can also be made with leftover turkey. It's best when piled with a few extra embellishments at serving time, such as sour cream, shredded cheese, raw onions, and even a handful of crushed corn chips.

Makes 6 to 8 servings

1½ cups dried beans, preferably a mix of pink and pintos, soaked overnight
2 tablespoons vegetable oil
1 large onion, chopped
2 large garlic cloves, minced
1 to 2 jalapeño peppers, minced
1 red bell pepper, diced
2 tablespoons chili powder
1½ teaspoons ground cumin
¾ teaspoon dried oregano
1 can (16 ounces) diced tomatoes
1 bottle (12 ounces) beer
2 teaspoons brown sugar
2½ cups cooked chicken or turkey, pulled into large shreds
Salt and cayenne
½ cup chopped fresh cilantro

---

1. Heat the oil in the pressure cooker over medium-high heat. Add the onion, garlic, and jalapeño peppers. Cook uncovered, stirring often, until onion begins to soften, 3 to 4 minutes. Add the bell pepper, chili powder, cumin, and oregano. Cook, stirring, 1 minute. Add the tomatoes with their liquid, beer, brown sugar, drained beans, and chicken.

2. Cover and bring up to high pressure. Reduce heat to stabilize pressure and cook 15 minutes. Release pressure. Season with salt and cayenne to taste. Stir in cilantro at serving time.

Last-Minute Turkey Chili

Ten minutes' preparation and five of cooking turn out a hearty and robust chili that also happens to be low in fat.

Makes 6 to 8 servings

1¼ pounds ground turkey
1 can (15 to 16 ounces) black beans, rinsed and drained
1 can (16 ounces) kidney beans, rinsed and drained
1 can (14½ ounces) Mexican-style stewed tomatoes
1 can (8 ounces) tomato sauce

½ cup beef stock or broth
2 tablespoons chili powder
1 small red bell pepper, diced
1 small onion, chopped
1 jalapeño or serrano pepper, minced
½ teaspoon salt
¼ teaspoon freshly ground pepper

Place ground turkey in the pressure cooker; break into chunks with a spoon. Add all remaining ingredients and mix well. Cover and bring up to high pressure. Reduce heat to stabilize pressure and cook 5 minutes. Release pressure.

Hungarian Beef and Pepper Goulash

This is a classic redefined for quick cooking in the pressure cooker. Serve the stew with boiled potatoes or spaetzle and rye bread.

Makes 4 to 6 servings

2 ounces smoked slab bacon, diced
1 large onion, cut in 1-inch pieces
1½ pounds beef stew meat, cut in
   1-inch cubes
2 medium green bell peppers, cut in
   1-inch squares
1 small red bell pepper, cut in 1-inch
   squares

½ cup dry vermouth
3 tablespoons tomato paste
1½ tablespoons sweet Hungarian
   paprika
Salt and freshly ground pepper
¼ cup sour cream

1. Cook the bacon in the pressure cooker uncovered over medium heat until crisp, 4 to 5 minutes. Add the onion and cook 1 minute. Add beef, raise heat to medium-high, and cook, turning, until beef is browned, 5 to 7 minutes. Add bell peppers.
2. Combine vermouth, tomato paste, and paprika in a small bowl; blend well. Add to cooker. Cover and bring up to high pressure. Reduce heat to stabilize pressure and cook 10 minutes. Release pressure. Season with salt and pepper, stir in sour cream, and serve.

Spanish Paella

The colors and flavors of this dish are enchanting, but what pleases and surprises even more is how quickly this complex dish can be prepared in the pressure cooker.

Makes 4 servings

2 garlic cloves, minced
1 tablespoon white wine vinegar
½ teaspoon hot paprika
½ teaspoon salt
¼ teaspoon freshly ground pepper
4 chicken thighs, skinned and boned
8 large shrimp, shelled and deveined
1 tablespoon olive oil
6 ounces spicy cured sausage, preferably Spanish chorizo or linguica, sliced

1 medium onion, minced
1¼ cups converted white rice
¼ cup dry vermouth
2 cups Chicken Stock (page 25) or canned broth
1 large tomato, seeded and chopped
¼ teaspoon saffron threads
¾ teaspoon dried marjoram
1 large roasted red bell pepper, diced
1 cup tiny frozen peas, thawed
¼ cup minced fresh cilantro or parsley

1. In a medium bowl, combine 1 minced garlic clove with vinegar, ¼ teaspoon paprika, salt, and pepper. Add chicken and shrimp; toss to mix. Cover and set aside for 30 minutes.

2. Heat the oil in the pressure cooker over medium-high heat. Add the sausage and cook uncovered until well browned; set aside with a slotted spoon. Add the chicken and shrimp to the pan. Cook, stirring often, until they are just cooked. Remove from cooker and set aside. Pour off all but 2 tablespoons fat.

3. Add remaining minced garlic clove and the onion. Cook, stirring, until onion begins to soften, 1 to 2 minutes. Add the rice and vermouth; boil until wine is almost cooked away. Add the stock or broth, tomato, saffron, marjoram, and remaining ¼ teaspoon paprika. Return chicken and shrimp to the pan and mix well.

4. Cover and bring up to high pressure. Reduce heat to stabilize pressure and cook 7 minutes. Release pressure by running cold water over the cover. Add the sausage, roasted pepper, peas, cilantro, salt, and pepper. Let stand, covered, 5 minutes.

Beef Carbonnade with Caramelized Onions

This Flemish pairing of beef with sweet, slow-cooked onions and beer is a classic. The bitter edge of beer is quieted by the natural sugar in the onions. In the pressure cooker, it is best to add the precooked onions toward the end of cooking so they don't become so soft that they dissolve into the sauce.

Makes 4 to 6 servings

---

2 tablespoons unsalted butter

2 large onions, cut in thin wedges

1 teaspoon dried thyme

1 teaspoon sugar

1½ teaspoons balsamic or red wine vinegar

2 strips of smoked bacon, diced

1½ pounds beef triangle tip roast, cut in 1-inch cubes

2 tablespoons all-purpose flour

1 cup beer, preferably a hearty ale

2 whole allspice berries

1 bay leaf

2 teaspoons honey mustard

Salt and freshly ground pepper

---

1. Melt the butter in the pressure cooker over medium-high heat. Add the onions and thyme. Cook uncovered, stirring often, 5 minutes. Sprinkle sugar over onions and reduce heat to medium-low. Cook, stirring occasionally, until the onions are very soft and lightly colored, 10 minutes longer. Stir in vinegar and remove from heat. Transfer onions to a bowl and set aside.

2. Add the bacon to the pressure cooker. Cook over medium heat until browned, 4 to 5 minutes. Remove with a slotted spoon and set aside. Raise heat to medium-high. Add beef to bacon drippings and cook, turning, until browned well, 5 to 7 minutes. Sprinkle on flour and cook, stirring, 1 minute. Add beer, bacon, allspice, and bay leaf.

3. Cover and bring up to high pressure. Reduce heat to stabilize pressure and cook 12 minutes. Release pressure and add the reserved onions. Cover again and return to high pressure. Cook 5 minutes. Release pressure and remove bay leaf. Blend in mustard and season with salt and pepper to taste.

Risotto Stew with Beef and Vegetables

Classic risotto is complicated by the last-minute cooking it requires. Though many occasions warrant such attention, here's an alternative that finds many of the same ingredients cooked into a stew.

Makes 4 to 6 servings

---

2 ounces pancetta, finely diced

1 tablespoon olive oil

6 ounces lean beef chuck, cut in small pieces

2 medium celery ribs, diced

2 large carrots, finely diced

2 cups shredded green or Savoy cabbage

1 tablespoon unsalted butter

¾ cup Arborio rice

¼ cup dry white wine or dry vermouth

1⅔ cups Chicken Stock (page 25) or canned broth

2 tablespoons tomato paste

2 teaspoons fresh rosemary or 1 teaspoon dried

Salt and freshly ground pepper

⅔ cup grated Parmesan cheese

---

1. Combine pancetta with oil in the pressure cooker. Cook uncovered over medium heat until the pancetta is brown and much of the fat is rendered, about 8 minutes. Add the beef and cook, stirring occasionally, until well browned, about 5 minutes. Remove pancetta and beef with a slotted spoon and set aside.

2. Add the celery, carrots, and cabbage to the pan. Cook 4 to 5 minutes, until softened. Add the butter, then the rice, stirring until the butter is melted. Add the wine. Raise the heat to high and boil until most of the liquid has evaporated. Add the stock or broth and tomato paste. Return the pancetta and beef to the pan. If you are using dried rosemary, add it now.

3. Cover and bring up to high pressure. Reduce heat to stabilize pressure and cook 6 minutes. Release the pressure. Unlock cover. Let rice stand, covered, 5 minutes. Add salt and pepper and fresh rosemary, if using. Pass the cheese separately.

Sonorran Green Chili

Although the list of ingredients for this chili is long, the preparation is simple and the cooking is quick. Corn muffins or warm flour tortillas are great to serve alongside.

Makes 8 to 10 servings

---

2 tablespoons vegetable oil
1 large onion, chopped
3 large garlic cloves, minced
4 teaspoons cumin seed
2 teaspoons ground oregano
1 pound ground beef
1 pound ground pork
1 pound lean beef stew meat, cut in
⅜-inch cubes
6 tablespoons all-purpose four

2 Anaheim peppers, diced
2 poblano peppers, diced
1 serrano pepper, minced
2 cans (4 ounces each) diced green
chiles, drained
2 cups Chicken Stock (page 25) or
canned broth
1 bottle (12 ounces) beer
Salt and freshly ground pepper
1 cup chopped cilantro

---

1. Heat the oil in the pressure cooker. Add the onion, garlic, cumin seed, and oregano. Cook uncovered over medium-high heat until the onion begins to soften, about 3 minutes. Add the meats and cook until well browned, about 10 minutes. Sprinkle flour over surface; stir in. Add peppers and canned chiles, stock or broth, and beer.

2. Cover and bring up to high pressure. Reduce heat to stabilize pressure and cook 8 minutes. Release pressure. Season with salt and pepper to taste. Stir in cilantro just before serving.

Beef and Vegetable Stew

Stew is almost infallible when it comes to adding warmth to a blustery day. This one, filled with beef and fresh-tasting vegetables in a rich, dark gravy, can be counted on to do the job quickly.

Makes 4 servings

2 tablespoons vegetable oil
1½ pounds beef chuck, cut in 1-inch cubes
2 tablespoons all-purpose flour
1 medium leek (white and tender green), bias-cut in 1-inch pieces
½ cup Beef Stock (page 26) or canned broth

1 can (8 ounces) tomato sauce
1 tablespoon Worcestershire sauce
1 teaspoon dried basil
3 medium carrots, bias-cut in ½-inch pieces
2 celery ribs, bias-cut in ½-inch pieces
1 cup tiny frozen peas, thawed
Salt and freshly ground pepper

1. Heat the oil in the pressure cooker over medium-high heat. Add the meat and cook uncovered, turning, until well browned, 6 to 8 minutes. Sprinkle on the flour and cook, stirring, 1 minute. Add the leek, beef stock, tomato sauce, Worcestershire sauce, and basil.

2. Cover and bring up to high pressure. Reduce heat to stabilize pressure and cook 10 minutes. Release pressure by running cold water over the cover. Add the carrots and celery. Cover and return pressure cooker to high pressure. Reduce heat and cook 5 minutes. Release pressure and add the peas. Season with salt and pepper to taste and serve.

Oxtail Stew with Root Vegetables

Oxtails can take as long as 3 hours to cook, and to those who savor the succulent bits of meat, it is time well spent. With the pressure cooker time is under three-quarters of an hour, making it all the more rewarding.

Makes 3 to 4 servings

1 tablespoon vegetable oil
2½ pounds oxtails
½ cup dry red wine
2 medium leeks (white and tender green), cut in ½-inch slices
3 carrots, cut in 1-inch pieces
1 medium celery root, peeled, cut in 1-inch pieces

2 tablespoons all-purpose flour
¾ cup Beef Stock (page 26) or canned broth
1 can (8 ounces) tomato sauce
2 bay leaves
¼ teaspoon celery seed
2 tablespoons minced fresh parsley
Salt and freshly ground pepper

1. Heat the oil in the pressure cooker. Add the oxtails and cook over high heat, turning, until well browned, 6 to 8 minutes. Pour the wine into the cooker and stir up any browned bits from the bottom of the pan. Add the leeks, carrots, and celery root. Sprinkle on the flour and stir in. Add the stock or broth, tomato sauce, bay leaves, and celery seed.

2. Cover and bring up to high pressure. Reduce heat to stabilize pressure and cook 30 minutes. Release pressure and skim fat from surface. Add the parsley and season with salt and pepper to taste.

White Beans with Escarole

Even as Americans explore seemingly every nuance of Italian cooking, this rustic regional dish remains overlooked by many. It is bold and fully flavored, yet makes no pretense to being anything other than a simple, characteristic peasant dish.

Makes 6 to 8 servings

1 cup navy beans, soaked overnight
2 tablespoons olive oil
2 to 3 large garlic cloves, minced
1⅔ cups Chicken Stock (page 25) or canned broth, or water
2 small dried red chiles

½ large bunch of escarole, about 8 ounces, cut in 1-inch pieces
1 large egg
½ cup grated Parmesan cheese
Salt and freshly ground pepper

1. Heat the oil in pressure cooker over medium heat. Add garlic and cook 2 minutes. Add the drained beans, stock, broth or water, and dried chiles.

2. Cover and bring up to high pressure. Reduce heat to stabilize pressure and cook 5 minutes. Release pressure by running cold water over the cover.

3. Add escarole and cover pressure cooker. Bring up to high pressure and remove from heat as soon as it is reached. Release pressure naturally.

4. Lightly whisk the egg in small mixing bowl. Stir in cheese. Slowly stir in about ½ cup of the liquid from the beans. Whisking as you do so, add the egg mixture to the beans. Cook uncovered over low heat, just until the mixture thickens. Season with salt and pepper to taste.

White Bean and Tuna Salad

Low in fat and packed with carbohydrates and protein, this salad packs well for brown bag lunches.

Makes 6 to 8 servings

---

2 cups navy beans, soaked overnight
5 cups water
⅓ cup olive oil
2 tablespoons red wine vinegar
2 tablespoons fresh lemon juice
¾ teaspoon dried tarragon
¼ teaspoon salt

⅛ teaspoon freshly ground pepper
4 scallions, thinly sliced
1 small tomato, seeded and diced
1 can (6 ounces) tuna, drained and flaked
2 tablespoons minced fresh parsley

---

1. Put the drained beans in the pressure cooker and add 5 cups fresh water. Cover and bring up to high pressure. Reduce heat to stabilize pressure and cook 5 minutes. Release pressure by running cold water over the cover.

2. Drain beans thoroughly and transfer to a mixing bowl. Add the oil, vinegar, lemon juice, tarragon, salt, and pepper while beans are warm; toss lightly and let cool.

3. Add scallions, tomato, tuna, and parsley; toss to mix. Serve warm or at room temperature.

Almost No-Fat Refried Beans

Low-fat, "guiltless" foods are wildly popular. This at-home version of a typically high-fat dish can be used as a side dish or dip, as a filling for burritos, or layered onto tortas or into tostadas. With lots of other flavors, the lard with its attendant fat and calories won't be missed a bit.

Makes 6 to 8 servings

1½ cups pinto beans, soaked overnight
2 garlic cloves, peeled
1 small onion, halved
4 cups water
2 tablespoons red wine vinegar
2 tablespoons sour cream or light sour cream, if desired

1 teaspoon chili powder, or more to taste
½ teaspoon ground cumin
Salt and cayenne

---

1. Put the drained beans, garlic, and onion in the pressure cooker and add 4 cups water. Cover and bring up to high pressure. Reduce heat to stabilize pressure and cook 10 minutes. Release pressure by running cold water over the cover. Drain well.
2. Mash contents of cooker with a potato masher. Add the vinegar, sour cream, chili powder, and cumin and blend well. Season with salt and cayenne to taste. To serve as a dip, puree in a food processor and thin the puree to the proper consistency with water, vegetable stock, or the cooking liquid reserved from the beans.

Bean Stew with Tomatoes, Spinach, and Mushrooms

Though robust and filling, perfect for a cold winter's day, this colorful casserole of beans and vegetables still conveys a light touch.

Makes 6 to 8 servings

2 cups navy pea beans, soaked
   overnight
4 cups water
1 to 2 tablespoons crushed hot pepper
   flakes
3 tablespoons olive oil
1 medium onion, chopped
2 garlic cloves, minced

6 ounces mushrooms, quartered
2 carrots, shredded
1½ teaspoons dried basil
1 can (16 ounces) diced tomatoes
1 box (10 ounces) frozen leaf spinach,
   thawed and squeezed dry
Salt and freshly ground pepper

1. Combine the drained beans, 4 cups of water, and hot pepper flakes in the pressure cooker. Cover and bring up to high pressure. Reduce heat to stabilize pressure and cook 5 minutes. Release pressure by running cold water over the cover. Drain beans and set aside.

2. Heat the oil in the pressure cooker over medium heat. Add the onion and garlic and cook uncovered until they begin to soften, 3 to 4 minutes. Add mushrooms, carrots, and basil; cook 2 minutes. Add beans, the tomatoes with their liquid, spinach, salt, and pepper.

3. Cover and bring up to high pressure. Reduce heat to stabilize pressure and cook 4 minutes. Release pressure.

Punjab Spiced Garbanzo Beans

In indian cooking, cauliflower is often cooked with tomatoes, peas, and a heady mix of spices. Here, in a heartier version, garbanzo beans replace the cauliflower. Serve it plain or over a bed of fragrant basmati rice.

Makes 6 to 8 servings

1 cup dried garbanzo beans, soaked
   overnight
2 tablespoons unsalted butter
1½ teaspoons mustard seeds
1 teaspoon cumin seeds
½ teaspoon ground coriander
Pinch of ground cardamom
2 large shallots, minced
2 garlic cloves, minced

1 fresh red hot pepper, minced
2 teaspoons minced fresh ginger
1 can (16 ounces) diced tomatoes
1½ cups water or Vegetable Stock
   (page 24)
1 cup tiny frozen peas, thawed
½ cup chopped fresh cilantro or
   parsley
Salt and cayenne

1. Melt the butter in the pressure cooker over medium-high heat. Add mustard seeds and cumin seeds, coriander, and cardamom. Cook uncovered, stirring often, until mustard seeds begin to pop, 3 to 4 minutes. Add the shallots, garlic, hot pepper, and ginger. Cook, stirring, 1 minute. Add drained garbanzo beans, the tomatoes with their liquid, and water or stock.

2. Cover and bring up to high pressure. Reduce heat to stabilize pressure and cook 12 minutes. Release pressure by running cold water over the cover. Mix in peas and cilantro or parsley. Season with salt and cayenne to taste.

Basic Lentils

Cooking lentils in the pressure cooker was once discouraged because they foam so much, leaving open the possibility of clogging the steam vent. It can be done quickly and successfully, though, with a little attention directed to the vent as they cook. If your cooker begins to clack or hiss loudly, release the pressure with cold water and check to see if the vent is clogged.

Makes 6 servings

---

1 cup brown, green, or red lentils   2 cups water
1 tablespoon vegetable oil   Salt

Combine the lentils, oil, and 2 cups water in the pressure cooker. Cover and bring up to high pressure. Reduce heat to stabilize pressure and cook red lentils for 3 to 4 minutes, brown or green lentils from 7 to 10 minutes. Timing varies. Release the pressure after the first cooking time indicated if you like lentils with a firm bite. Cook longer for more tender lentils. Release pressure by running cold water over the lid. Drain well and add salt to taste.

Lentil and Rice Pilaf

Lentils added to a simple rice pilaf contribute substance and their unique peppery taste. Grilled lamb or chicken are good accompaniments, though there may be times when a salad and the pilaf make a meal.

Makes 6 to 8 servings

1 cup converted white rice
⅔ cup brown or green lentils
3 cups Vegetable Stock (page 24) or
　broth

1 jalapeño or serrano pepper, minced
½ teaspoon curry powder
Salt and freshly ground pepper

1. Combine the rice, lentils, stock, jalapeño pepper, and curry powder in the pressure cooker. Cover and bring up to high pressure. Reduce heat to stabilize pressure and cook 8 minutes for tender-firm lentils or up to 10 minutes for soft lentils. Release pressure by running cold water over the cover.

2. Unlock cover; leave it in place and let pilaf stand for 5 minutes. Season with salt and pepper to taste.

Indian Lentil Dal

Dal, *the Indian word for lentils, also refers to a preparation of spiced pureed lentils. Those who like the peppery bite of lentils will easily be seduced by this rich and soothing dish.*

Makes 6 servings

---

1 cup brown or green lentils	¼ teaspoon turmeric
1 tablespoon vegetable oil	¼ teaspoon mustard seeds
2 cups water	¼ teaspoon cayenne
2 tablespoons unsalted butter	1 small tomato, seeded and chopped
1½ teaspoons minced fresh ginger	¾ cup Vegetable Stock (page 24) or
1 small jalapeño or serrano pepper,	canned broth
minced (optional)	⅓ cup whipping cream
½ teaspoon ground cumin	Salt

---

1. Combine the lentils, oil, and 2 cups water in the pressure cooker. Cover and bring up to high pressure. Reduce heat to stabilize pressure and cook 8 minutes. Release pressure by running cold water over the cover. Drain lentils and set aside.
2. Melt the butter in the pressure cooker over medium heat. Add the ginger, hot pepper, cumin, turmeric, mustard seeds, and cayenne. Cook uncovered, stirring often, until fragrant, 1 to 2 minutes. Add the cooked lentils, tomato, stock, and cream.
3. Cover and bring up to high pressure. Reduce heat to stabilize pressure and cook 5 minutes. Release pressure. Stir with a large spoon to break up the lentils into a rough puree. Season with salt to taste.

Lentil Slaw

The peppery taste of lentils is an unexpected addition to a vegetable slaw. To suit the changing seasons, serve this hot or chilled and vary the herbs.

Makes 6 servings

1 cup brown or green lentils
3 tablespoons vegetable oil
3 cups water
2 tablespoons seasoned rice vinegar
1 cup finely chopped red cabbage
1 cup finely chopped green cabbage
1 large carrot, peeled and finely chopped

½ cup chopped fresh fennel bulb or 2 celery ribs, chopped
2 scallions, sliced
Florets from 1 small broccoli stalk
½ cup mixed fresh herbs (such as mint, cilantro, and basil), chopped
Salt and freshly ground pepper

1. Combine the lentils, 1 tablespoon oil, and 3 cups water in the pressure cooker. Cover and bring up to high pressure. Reduce heat to stabilize pressure and cook 7 to 10 minutes. Timing varies: Start testing at 7 minutes. To test, release pressure by running cold water over the lid. Lentils should be firm.
2. Drain the lentils thoroughly, shaking the colander to remove as much water as possible. Transfer to a mixing bowl and add the remaining 2 tablespoons oil and the vinegar; toss to combine. Add the red cabbage, green cabbage, carrot, fennel, scallions, broccoli, and herbs and mix gently. Season with salt and pepper to taste. Serve warm or chilled.

Rice and Grains

The nutritional call to eat more complex carbohydrates keeps getting easier to respond to, thanks in part to the growing family of rice and grains. The variety of types generally available, from amaranth to rice to quinoa, continues to expand, so there are more choices to tempt our taste buds. And with the pressure cooker, cooking is quick, thus eliminating the last-minute lament that there's not enough time to add these nutritional powerhouses to a menu.

White rice is arguably the most popular of the cereal grains on the American table. The ongoing debate about which route to choose for perfectly cooked fluffy white grains can end right here. The pressure cooker takes on the task with its usual unfussy skill. As to what type of white rice to use, there are lots of alternatives to long-grain white rice. Americans have caught on to some imported secrets. Thai jasmine rice is fragrant and delicious. Indian basmati, and its American counterpart called Texmati have an exotic edge. Italian Arborio, with its plump, pearl-white kernels, is the basis for risotto.

While rice is king in many parts of the world, wheat is the most popular grain in America, thanks to bread. But whole wheat berries are unusual and delicious. Without a pressure cooker, they take at least 4 hours to cook. I soak them overnight, then cook them in a mere 10 minutes. Other great grains include the brown rice family, millet, wehani (a type of rice), kasha, barley, and couscous.

The biggest conundrum about rice and grains comes as you ponder what to use the pressure cooker for: main dish or side dish. That's when you may decide you want two pressure cookers in the kitchen.

Hints and tips:
- When cooking rice and grains, never fill the cooker more than halfway.
- Standing time at the end of cooking finishes the process. Don't shortcut this step.
- Time rice and grains carefully. Since they absorb liquid, the cooker will be fairly dry toward the end of cooking. An extra minute or two of heat will lead to burning.
- In pressure cookers with a removable pressure regulator, you may find that you need slightly more liquid in rice and grain cookery.

Basic White Rice

There are many uses for plain cooked rice and just as many ways to jazz it up. Fresh herbs, spices, and aromatics can be added. The cooking liquid can be varied, and many things can be added—literally from soup to nuts.

Makes 4 servings

---

1 cup converted white rice

2 cups water, Chicken Stock (page 25) or broth, or Vegetable Stock (page 24)

1 tablespoon unsalted butter, if desired

Salt and freshly ground pepper

---

1. Combine all ingredients in the pressure cooker. Cover and bring up to high pressure. Reduce heat to stabilize pressure and cook 7 minutes.

2. Release pressure by running cold water over the cover. Let stand, covered, 5 minutes.

Four-Grain Pilaf

Pasta made from wheat mixes with rice, millet, and barley in a pilaf that is sturdy in character, yet delicate in taste.

Makes 6 to 8 servings

---

1 tablespoon unsalted butter
1 large shallot, minced
1 garlic clove, minced
½ cup pearl barley
½ cup converted white rice
½ cup orzo pasta

2 tablespoons millet
3¼ cups Chicken Stock (page 25) or
canned broth, or Vegetable Stock
(page 24)
Salt and freshly ground pepper

---

1. Melt the butter in the pressure cooker. Add the shallot and garlic and cook uncovered over medium heat until they begin to soften, 2 to 3 minutes. Stir in barley, rice, pasta, and millet; cook 1 minute. Add stock or broth.

2. Cover and bring up to high pressure. Reduce heat to stabilize pressure and cook 12 minutes. Release pressure and unlock cover. Let stand for 5 minutes with the cover on. Season with salt and pepper to taste and serve.

Aztec Rice

This is a perfect companion to Mexican or Spanish meals.

Makes 4 to 6 servings

---

2 ounces chorizo sausage, removed
    from casing
2 Anaheim peppers, seeded and finely
    diced
½ small onion, diced

1 garlic clove, minced
1 cup converted white rice
2 cups Chicken Stock (page 25) or
    canned broth
Salt and freshly ground pepper

---

1. In uncovered pressure cooker, combine the sausage with peppers, onion, and garlic. Cook over medium-high heat until the onion is softened and the sausage is lightly browned, 3 to 5 minutes. Add the rice and stock or broth.

2. Cover and bring up to high pressure. Reduce heat to stabilize pressure and cook 7 minutes. Release pressure. Let rice stand, covered, for 3 to 4 minutes. Season with salt and pepper to taste and serve.

Greek Rice with Pasta

Tangy with lemon and enlivened with bits of arugula, this pasta and rice combo can be served with grilled fish or poultry.

Makes 4 to 6 servings

---

2 tablespoons olive oil
1 teaspoon dried oregano
¼ teaspoon dried mint
⅔ cup converted white rice
⅓ cup orzo pasta
1 garlic clove, minced
2 teaspoons grated lemon zest

2 cups Chicken Stock (page 25) or canned broth
1 tablespoon fresh lemon juice
⅓ cup packed chopped arugula or watercress
Salt and freshly ground pepper

---

1. Heat the oil in the pressure cooker over high heat. Add the oregano, mint, rice, and pasta. Cook, stirring often, until the rice is golden, 4 to 5 minutes. Add the garlic and lemon zest and cook 30 seconds. Add the stock or broth.

2. Cover and bring up to high pressure. Reduce heat to stabilize pressure and cook 7 minutes. Release pressure and unlock cover. Let stand with cover on but not locked for 5 minutes. Add the lemon juice and arugula or watercress. Season with salt and pepper to taste.

Wheat Berry and Basmati Rice Medley

Basmati is an especially fragrant variety of rice that blends with many ingredients and flavors, including this unexpected partnership with little nuggets of wheat. Herbs and spices can be added to tailor the side dish to a particular meal.

Makes 6 servings

½ cup wheat berries
1 tablespoon unsalted butter
1 small onion, chopped
¾ cup basmati or Texmati rice

2½ cups Vegetable Stock (page 24) or
  water
Salt and freshly ground pepper

---

1. Soak the wheat berries in water overnight; drain.

2. Melt the butter in the pressure cooker. Add the onion and cook uncovered over medium-high heat until it begins to brown at the edges, about 3 minutes. Add the wheat berries, rice, and stock or water.

3. Cover and bring up to high pressure. Reduce heat to stabilize pressure and cook 7 minutes. Release pressure and let stand, covered, for 5 minutes. Season with salt and pepper to taste.

Basic Brown Rice

With the bran and hull layers left intact, brown rice has significantly more fiber than white rice. Besides, it has a delicious, nutty taste, reason enough to add it to your menus. Be sure to store brown rice in your refrigerator or freezer to keep it fresh-tasting.

Makes 4 servings

---

1 cup long-grain brown rice	1 tablespoon unsalted butter, if desired
1¾ cups water or Vegetable Stock	½ teaspoon salt
(page 24)	⅛ teaspoon freshly ground pepper

Combine all ingredients in the pressure cooker. Cover and bring up to high pressure. Reduce heat to stabilize pressure and cook 18 minutes. Release pressure by running cold water over the cover. Let stand, covered, for 5 minutes.

Brown Rice with Spicy Browned Onions

Sweet onions are a fine foil for the little nip that comes from hot pepper jelly. The jellies vary in degrees, so add the amount accordingly.

Makes 6 servings

---

2 medium onions, cut in half
   crosswise
2½ tablespoons unsalted butter
1 to 2 tablespoons hot pepper jelly or
   jalapeño jelly
1 cup long-grain brown rice

1¾ cups water
½ teaspoon ground cumin
½ teaspoon grated orange zest
½ teaspoon salt
¼ teaspoon freshly ground pepper

---

1. Cut each onion half into ½-inch wedges. Melt 2 tablespoons butter in the pressure cooker over high heat. Add the onions and cook uncovered, stirring often, until they begin to brown at the edges, 4 to 5 minutes. Reduce heat to medium and continue cooking until the onions are golden and tender, 10 to 12 minutes. Add the jelly, stirring until it melts. Remove onions from cooker and set aside.

2. Add the rice, water, cumin, orange zest, and remaining ½ tablespoon butter to cooker. Cover and bring up to full pressure. Reduce heat to stabilize pressure and cook 20 minutes. Release pressure. Stir in onions and season with salt and pepper.

Brown Rice with Forty Shades of Green

Just as it seems the Emerald Isle has a full palette of green tones, so too with this simple rice dish. For the easiest preparation, chop the greens in a food processor.

Makes 4 to 6 servings

1¾ cups water or Vegetable Stock (page 24)
1 cup brown rice
1 teaspoon salt
4 scallions, chopped
6 ounces tender leaf spinach, stems removed, finely chopped
1 cup parsley sprigs, chopped

½ cup fresh basil leaves, chopped
½ cup cilantro or mint leaves, chopped
⅛ teaspoon freshly ground pepper
2 to 3 tablespoons sour cream, if desired

---

1. Combine the water or broth, rice, and salt in the pressure cooker. Cover and bring up to high pressure. Reduce heat to stabilize pressure and cook 18 minutes. Release pressure and let stand, covered, 5 minutes.

2. Add all the remaining ingredients and mix well. Serve hot or at room temperature.

Risotto with Seared Asparagus and Smoked Mozzarella

Rich and elegant, this may be served as a first course or as a springtime entree.

Makes 4 to 6 servings

---

1 pound slender asparagus
1½ tablespoons olive oil
Salt
1 tablespoon unsalted butter
1 cup Arborio rice
¼ cup dry white wine

2¼ cups Chicken Stock (page 25) or
    canned broth
½ cup shredded smoked mozzarella
    cheese (or other smoked cheese)
Freshly ground pepper
Grated Parmesan cheese, for serving

---

1. Cut off the bottom third of the asparagus. Cut the remainder of the spears into ¾-inch pieces and reserve. Finely mince the bottom third.

2. Heat the oil with a dash of salt in the pressure cooker over high heat. Add the asparagus pieces. Cook uncovered over high heat, shaking the pan occasionally, until the asparagus is beginning to brown at the edges, 4 to 5 minutes. Remove from the cooker and set aside. (If your pressure cooker is lightweight aluminum, you will have better results browning the asparagus in a heavy skillet.)

3. Let the pressure cooker cool for a minute, then add the butter. Return to medium heat and add the rice. Stir so it is well coated with butter. Add the wine and boil over high heat until it almost has evaporated. Add the minced asparagus stems and stock or broth.

4. Cover and bring up to high pressure. Reduce heat to stabilize pressure and cook 6 minutes. Release pressure by running cold water over the cover. Add reserved asparagus and smoked mozzarella cheese. Cover pressure cooker and let stand 5 minutes. Season with salt and pepper to taste. Serve at once, with Parmesan cheese on the side.

Wild Mushroom Risotto

This is an exquisitely orchestrated dish, combining the justly famous Italian rice with a forager's treasure. Do try, as cost and availability allow, to have at least one type of exotic mushroom included in the mix.

Makes 2 to 4 servings

½ pound mixed wild mushrooms, such
    as chanterelles, porcini, and cremini
2 tablespoons olive oil
½ teaspoon fresh or dried rosemary
Salt and freshly ground pepper
1 tablespoon unsalted butter

1 large shallot, minced
1 cup Arborio rice
¼ cup dry white wine
2¼ cups Chicken Stock (page 25) or
    canned broth
Grated Parmesan cheese, for serving

---

1. Trim the stems from the mushrooms and chop fine. Slice the caps.

2. Heat the oil in the pressure cooker over high heat. Add the sliced mushroom caps, a pinch of the rosemary, ¼ teaspoon salt, and ⅛ teaspoon pepper. Cook uncovered, stirring, until the mushrooms begin to soften, about 3 minutes. Remove from cooker and set aside.

3. Add the butter to the cooker. When it melts, add the shallot and chopped mushroom stems. Cook 2 minutes. Add the rice and stir so it is well coated with butter. Add the wine and stir up the browned bits from the bottom of the pan. Add the stock or broth and the remaining rosemary.

4. Cover and bring up to high pressure. Reduce heat to stabilize pressure and cook 6 minutes. Release pressure by running cold water over the lid. Add the mushroom caps and cover cooker but do not lock. Let stand for 5 minutes. Season with additional salt and pepper to taste and serve at once, with grated Parmesan cheese on the side.

Wehani Mexicani

Wehani is a variety of rice that looks like a cross between brown and wild rice. It has a dark, reddish brown coating and a nutty taste and aroma. Here, it is prepared in a Mexican style.

Makes 4 to 6 servings

---

2 slices of smoked bacon, diced
½ small onion, chopped
2 teaspoons chili powder
¼ teaspoon ground coriander
1 cup wehani rice

2 cups water
⅔ cup corn kernels
1 scallion, thinly sliced
¼ cup minced fresh cilantro
Salt and freshly ground pepper

---

1. Cook the bacon uncovered in the pressure cooker over medium heat until it is browned and most of the fat is rendered, about 5 minutes. Remove bacon with a slotted spoon and set aside. Add the onion, chili powder, and coriander to the drippings and cook for 30 seconds. Add the rice and cook 1 minute longer. Add water. **2.** Cover and bring up to high pressure. Reduce heat and cook 20 minutes. Release pressure. Rice should be tender; if not, cover pressure cooker and return to high pressure, adding a small amount of water if it has all cooked away. Add additional time as necessary. Stir in the bacon, corn, scallion, and cilantro. Season with salt and pepper to taste.

Calypso Rice and Beans

This colorful island-inspired dish is made with canned black beans for convenience's sake. Two cups of cooked dried black beans can be used in place of canned beans.

Makes 6 servings

---

1 tablespoon vegetable oil
1 small onion, chopped
½ small red bell pepper, finely diced
½ small green bell pepper, finely diced
1 jalapeño or serrano pepper, minced
1 cup converted white rice
1¼ cups water or Vegetable Stock
   (page 24)

¾ cup unsweetened coconut milk
1 can (16 ounces) black beans, rinsed
   and drained
¼ cup chopped fresh cilantro or
   parsley
Salt

---

1. Heat the oil in the pressure cooker. Add the onion, red and green bell peppers, and hot pepper. Cook uncovered over medium-high heat, stirring occasionally, until vegetables begin to brown at the edges, 5 minutes. Add rice, water or broth, and coconut milk.
2. Cover and bring up to high pressure. Reduce heat to stabilize pressure and cook 7 minutes. Release pressure and unlock cover. Add beans. Let stand with cover on for 5 minutes. Stir in the cilantro or parsley and salt to taste.

Toasted Millet Pilaf

Millet may be most familiar to some as a chief component of birdseed, but the little golden pellets are a welcome addition to the family of grains. This simple preparation can be served in place of rice.

Makes 4 servings

---

1 tablespoon vegetable oil
1 cup millet
1⅔ cups Chicken Stock (page 25) or
   broth, Vegetable Stock (page 24) or
   water

Salt and freshly ground pepper

---

1. Heat the oil in the pressure cooker over high heat. When it is hot, add millet. Cook uncovered, stirring often, until the millet is lightly toasted and fragrant, 3 to 4 minutes. Add stock, broth, or water.
2. Cover and bring up to high pressure. Reduce heat to stabilize pressure and cook 7 minutes. Release pressure. Let stand, covered, 5 minutes. Season with salt and pepper to taste.

Wheat Berry Tabbouleh

This refreshing Middle Eastern salad usually is made with cracked wheat berries, or bulgur. This time, it's chewy whole grains of wheat that make up the substance.

Makes 3 to 4 servings

½ cup wheat berries

2 garlic cloves, minced

1 small serrano or jalapeño pepper, seeded and minced

2 tablespoons olive oil

1¾ tablespoons fresh lemon juice

¼ teaspoon salt

⅛ teaspoon freshly ground pepper

1 cup watercress leaves

½ cup cilantro sprigs or parsley

2 tablespoons fresh mint leaves, if desired

2 scallions, thinly sliced

1 large tomato, finely diced

---

1. Soak the wheat berries in water overnight; drain. Put in the pressure cooker with 1½ cups water. Cover and bring up to high pressure. Reduce heat to stabilize pressure and cook 10 minutes. Release pressure. Drain berries thoroughly.

2. Combine the garlic, hot pepper, oil, lemon juice, salt, and pepper in a medium bowl. Chop the watercress, cilantro, and mint together. Add to the bowl along with the wheat berries, scallions, and tomato. Mix well. Serve at room temperature or chilled.

Wild Rice with Pecans and Dried Cranberries

Wild rice, actually a grass rather than a grain, is a distinctly American ingredient. Preparing it with other traditional American ingredients, such as bourbon and cranberries, honors this heritage.

Makes 6 servings

¼ cup dried cranberries, chopped
1 tablespoon bourbon (optional)
3 tablespoons unsalted butter
½ cup chopped pecans
2 shallots, minced

1 cup wild rice
2¼ cups Beef Stock (page 26) or
  canned broth
Salt and freshly ground pepper

---

1. Combine the cranberries and bourbon in a small plastic food bag; seal and set aside for at least 20 minutes. The cranberries can be softened in water instead of bourbon, if preferred.

2. Melt the butter in the pressure cooker. Add pecans and cook uncovered over medium heat until they are lightly toasted, 2 minutes. Remove with a slotted spoon and set aside. Add the shallots; cook, stirring, until softened and fragrant, about 1 minute. Add the rice and stock or broth.

3. Cover and bring up to high pressure. Reduce heat to stabilize pressure and cook 21 minutes. Rice should be firm but tender. Add more time if necessary. If there is stock left when the rice is fully cooked, drain well. Stir in the pecans and cranberries. Season with salt and pepper to taste.

Barley and Vegetable Pilaf

Barley extends its sturdy taste and character to a host of vegetables in this colorful pilaf. It can be served with simple grilled or roasted meat or poultry or partnered with a salad and served as a light main course.

Makes 6 servings

2½ tablespoons unsalted butter
¼ cup chopped pecans
1 small onion, minced
1 medium carrot, finely diced
1 celery rib, finely diced
¼ pound cultivated or wild mush-
    rooms, finely diced

1 cup chopped green cabbage
¼ teaspoon salt
⅛ teaspoon freshly ground pepper
1 cup pearl barley
2½ cups Beef Stock (page 26) or
    canned broth
2 tablespoons minced parsley

---

1. Melt 1 tablespoon of the butter in the pressure cooker over medium-high heat. Add the pecans and cook uncovered, stirring often, until they are browned and fragrant, 3 to 4 minutes. Remove with a slotted spoon and set aside.

2. Melt the remaining 1½ tablespoons butter in the cooker. Add onion and carrot and cook until they begin to soften, about 3 minutes. Add the celery and mushrooms. Cook until the vegetables are crisp-tender, about 3 minutes longer. Transfer to a medium bowl and add cabbage, salt, and pepper.

3. Add the barley and stock or broth to cooker. Cover and bring up to high pressure. Reduce heat to stabilize pressure and cook 15 minutes. Release pressure by running cold water over the cover. Add the vegetables and return to high pressure. Immediately remove from heat and release pressure. Add the pecans and parsley and toss to mix.

Vegetables

Vegetables are delicate, they cook quickly, and every cook already has a whole slate of simple preparations for them. So why use the pressure cooker to ready vegetables for the table? Simply put, because it does a spectacular job. Vegetables emerge from the pressure cooker with vibrant color, perfect texture, and lots of their nutrients intact, since they cook in a tightly sealed vessel.

Cookbook author Shirley Conran gets the credit for penning the sentiment that "Life is too short to stuff a mushroom," but it could have been I. It pretty well sums up my approach to cooking vegetables. Straightforward, unfussy preparations most often show them off to their best advantage. When vegetables are at their peak of freshness, there's no need to spend a lot of time and effort with extravagant recipes. Most of the recipes here strive for simplicity and speed.

Each season offers it own bounty. Much is made of the summer harvest, and I am the first one to revel in the lush abundance and the array of warm-weather choices. But a winter produce bin still pleases me. Sturdier stalwarts like potatoes, winter squash, carrots, turnips, and broccoli fill the market, and I take pleasure in their richer, deeper tastes and their strength of character, so welcome during colder months.

Hints and tips:

- For even cooking make sure vegetables are the same size or are cut the same size.
- In almost all recipes in the following chapter, timing starts as soon as the cooker is placed over high heat instead of when high pressure is attained. This accommodates the vegetables' short cooking time and gives more control.
- In recipes where several types of vegetables are combined, cut harder items such as potatoes, turnips, and winter squash into smaller pieces than softer ones, since the harder ones take longer to cook. In some cases, it may be preferable to cook harder types for several minutes before adding the softer items.
- Timing is critical. One minute too long can turn perfectly cooked broccoli into a candidate for pureeing, so watch the clock.
- For delicate vegetables, such as asparagus and green beans, you may wish to rinse them under cold water as soon as they are done to halt the cooking immediately.

Provençal Artichoke Ragout

When the cost of artichokes plummets in the spring, this is a superb way to enjoy the bounty. Serve in soup bowls, with the broth.

Makes 4 servings

---

2 jumbo artichokes
1½ tablespoons olive oil
1 slice of Canadian bacon, finely diced
1 shallot, minced
1 small garlic clove, minced
¼ teaspoon dried thyme
¼ teaspoon dried oregano
1½ teaspoons all-purpose flour

½ cup dry white wine
⅓ cup Chicken Stock (page 25) or
  canned broth
1 tablespoon red wine vinegar or
  sherry vinegar
1 strip of orange zest, about 2 inches,
  removed with a vegetable peeler
Salt and freshly ground pepper

---

1. Trim about 1 inch from the top of each artichoke and the dried end of the stem. Remove tough outer leaves and trim the pointed tips. Cut each artichoke in half lengthwise and cut away the fuzzy choke from the center. Set aside.
2. Heat the oil in the pressure cooker over medium-high heat. Add the bacon, shallot, garlic, thyme, and oregano. Cook uncovered, stirring often, until the shallot and garlic are soft, 2 to 3 minutes. Sprinkle on the flour and cook, stirring, 1 minute. Stir in the wine, stock or broth, vinegar, and orange zest. Add the artichokes.
3. Cover the pressure cooker. Start timing immediately and cook exactly 5 minutes. Release pressure by running cold water over the lid. Season with salt and pepper to taste and serve.

Pan-Asian Asparagus Stew

A diverse collection of cultural influences contributes to this deliciously colorful springtime fling.

Makes 3 to 4 servings

2½ tablespoons unsalted butter
1 poblano or Anaheim pepper, cut into ½-inch dice
1 small red bell pepper, cut into ½-inch dice
1 small yellow bell pepper, cut into ½-inch dice
1 medium shallot, minced
1 small leek (white part only), sliced

1 pound asparagus, ends trimmed, cut into 1-inch pieces
1 cup Chicken Stock (page 25) or canned broth, or Vegetable Stock (page 24)
1 teaspoon grated orange zest
¼ cup minced fresh basil
1 tablespoon seasoned rice vinegar
Salt and freshly ground pepper

---

1. Melt the butter in the pressure cooker over high heat. Add the peppers, shallot, and leek. Cook uncovered, stirring often, until peppers begin to brown at the edges, 4 to 5 minutes. Add the asparagus, stock or broth, and orange zest.

2. Cover and place over high heat. Start timing immediately and cook 3 minutes. Release pressure by running cold water over the cover.

3. Return to high heat and boil uncovered 2 minutes to reduce the liquid. Remove from heat and stir in the basil, vinegar, and salt and pepper to taste.

Beet Puree with Carrots and Apple

Dramatically colored, this deep garnet puree is especially good alongside pork or poached fish.

Makes 6 servings

---

1 tablespoon unsalted butter

1 large tart apple, peeled, cored, and sliced

4 medium beets (about 12 ounces) peeled and thinly sliced

2 large carrots (about 12 ounces), peeled and thinly sliced

½ cup apple cider

½ cup Vegetable Stock (page 24) or canned broth

2 tablespoons cider vinegar

¼ cup sour cream

¼ teaspoon salt

---

1. Melt the butter in the pressure cooker. Add the apple and cook uncovered over medium heat until it begins to brown at the edges, 3 minutes. Add the beets, carrots, apple cider, stock or broth, and vinegar.

2. Cover and bring up to high heat. Reduce heat to stabilize pressure and cook 10 minutes. Release pressure.

3. With a slotted spoon, transfer vegetables and apple to a blender or food processor. Return the liquid in pressure cooker to high heat. Boil uncovered until thick and syrupy, 3 to 4 minutes. Pour into the blender or processor, add sour cream and salt, and puree until smooth.

Broccoli with Parmesan Cheese

Vegetables often require two-step cooking—first a preliminary blanching followed by a quick finish in a hot skillet. The same technique adapted to the pressure cooker results in a simple preparation for broccoli. If the broccoli stems are tough, peel the outer layer with a vegetable peeler.

Makes 2 to 3 servings

---

1 pound broccoli, cut into large spears
1½ tablespoons olive oil
Pinch of crushed hot pepper flakes

2 tablespoons grated Parmesan cheese
Salt

---

1. Combine the broccoli and 1 cup of water in the pressure cooker. Cover and place over high heat. Start timing immediately and cook 5 minutes. Release pressure by running cold water over the lid.

2. Drain the broccoli. Wipe pressure cooker dry. Add the oil and hot pepper flakes and place over high heat. When the oil is hot, add the broccoli. Cook uncovered, shaking pan often, until the broccoli begins to brown at the edges, 3 to 4 minutes. Transfer to a serving dish and sprinkle with the cheese and salt to taste.

Brussels Sprouts with Lemon-Lime Butter

Sprightly citrus tastes enliven the taste of brussels sprouts, while little bits of red pepper add a dash of color. Be sure to use just the zest, the colored part of the citrus peel; the spongy white pith can be bitter.

Makes 4 to 6 servings

¾ cup Chicken Stock (page 25) or
    canned broth
2 teaspoons honey mustard
½ teaspoon minced lemon zest
½ teaspoon minced lime zest
½ teaspoon dried thyme

1½ pounds brussels sprouts, trimmed
¼ cup very finely diced red bell pepper
2 tablespoons unsalted butter
1 teaspoon fresh lime juice
Dash of cayenne
Salt

1. Combine the stock or broth, mustard, lemon zest, lime zest, and thyme in the pressure cooker. Stir to blend in mustard. Add brussels sprouts.

2. Cover the pressure cooker. Start timing immediately and cook for 6 minutes. Release pressure by running cold water over the cover. Add the bell pepper, butter, lime juice, cayenne, and salt to taste. Serve at once.

Curried Cabbage and Apples

Apples have a special affinity for cabbage. Their sweet/tart flavor softens its earthy taste and readies it for robust seasonings. The curry here is a blend of several spices, rather than the usual premixed powder. Add cayenne to your liking, going anywhere from mildly spiced to potently hot.

Makes 6 servings

2 tablespoons unsalted butter	Pinch of ground turmeric
1 medium onion, diced	¾ cup Chicken Stock (page 25) or
2 teaspoons minced fresh ginger	canned broth
1½ pounds green cabbage, shredded	¾ teaspoon salt
1 large tart apple, peeled and shredded	⅛ to ½ teaspoon cayenne
½ teaspoon ground cumin	1 tablespoon cider vinegar
Pinch of cinnamon	¼ cup minced cilantro or parsley

1. Melt the butter in the pressure cooker over medium-high heat. Add the onion and cook uncovered until it begins to brown at the edges, about 5 minutes. Add ginger and cook 30 seconds. Add the cabbage, apple, cumin, cinnamon, turmeric, stock or broth, salt, and cayenne.

2. Cover and bring up to high pressure. Reduce heat to stabilize pressure and cook 3 minutes. Release pressure. Mix in vinegar and serve sprinkled with cilantro or parsley.

Red on Red Cabbage

This crimson dish is especially good with roast pork or turkey. Be sure to cut the red cabbage with a stainless steel knife to prevent discoloration.

Makes 4 servings

---

1 tablespoon unsalted butter
1 small red onion, cut in thin wedges
1 medium beet, peeled and cut in thin strips
1 small head of red cabbage (1 pound), cut in ½-inch ribbons
¼ cup port wine

¼ cup raspberry or cider vinegar
3 tablespoons chutney
1 tablespoon brown sugar
⅛ teaspoon ground allspice
¾ teaspoon salt
¼ teaspoon freshly ground pepper

---

1. Melt the butter in the pressure cooker. Add the onion and cook uncovered over medium heat until it begins to soften, about 2 minutes. Add the beet, cabbage, wine, vinegar, chutney, brown sugar, allspice, salt, and pepper.
2. Cover and place over high heat. Start timing immediately and cook 10 minutes. Release pressure by running cold water over the cover.

Honey-Glazed Carrots with Balsamic Vinegar

Almost all markets now stock packages of fresh baby carrots that are peeled, trimmed, and ready to snack on or cook with.

Makes 4 to 6 servings

---

1 pound ready-cut whole baby carrots
¾ cup Chicken Stock (page 25) or
   canned broth, or Vegetable Stock
   (page 24)
2 tablespoons unsalted butter

1 medium shallot, minced
1½ tablespoons balsamic vinegar
1 tablespoon honey
¾ teaspoon crushed dried rosemary
Salt and freshly ground pepper

---

1. Combine the carrots, stock or broth, 1 tablespoon butter, and shallot in the pressure cooker. Cover and place over high heat. Start timing immediately and cook 8 minutes. Release pressure by running cold water over the lid.

2. Add the vinegar, honey, and rosemary. Boil over high heat until liquid is syrupy and coats the carrots, 6 to 7 minutes. Toss with the remaining 1 tablespoon butter and season with salt and pepper to taste.

Mashed Celery Root with Turnips and Apples

Though it is hard to tell from its gnarled and hairy exterior, celery root (also called celeriac or knob celery) has creamy white flesh with a delicate taste. It mixes well with other seasonal favorites. Besides turnips, try parsnips or potatoes.

Makes 4 servings

---

2 medium-sized, smooth celery roots, peeled and sliced

2 medium turnips, peeled and sliced

1 large apple, peeled, cored, and cut in chunks

1 cup Chicken Stock (page 25), Vegetable Stock (page 24), or water

3 tablespoons whipping cream

1 tablespoon unsalted butter

⅛ teaspoon freshly grated nutmeg

Salt and freshly ground pepper

---

1. Combine the celery roots, turnips, apple, and stock or water in the pressure cooker. Cover and bring up to high pressure. Reduce heat to stabilize pressure and cook 7 minutes. Release pressure.

2. Drain and place cooker over low heat for 1 minute to dry excess moisture. Puree in a food processor or blender with the cream, butter, and nutmeg. Season with salt and pepper to taste.

Summer Corn with Zucchini and Tomatoes

This quick, simple preparation flatters the best of a summer garden.

Makes 6 to 8 servings

---

2 large ears of sweet corn, shucked
2 tablespoons unsalted butter
⅔ cup Chicken Stock (page 25) or
  canned broth, or Vegetable Stock
  (page 24)
4 to 5 small zucchini, sliced

2 medium red bell peppers, diced
2 large tomatoes, diced
2 tablespoons chopped fresh basil or
  1½ teaspoons dried
Pinch of cayenne
Salt

---

1. With a large knife, cut the corn kernels off the cob. Melt the butter in the pressure cooker. Add the stock or broth, corn, zucchini, bell peppers, tomatoes, and dried basil, if using.

2. Cover and place over high heat. Start timing immediately and cook 4 minutes. Release the pressure by running cold water over the cover. Toss with fresh basil, cayenne, and salt to taste.

Chinese Curry-Braised Eggplant

With its neutral flavor, eggplant avidly takes on the character of the spices used to season it. Many combinations work well, but this one is especially complex and pleasing.

Makes 4 servings

---

2 tablespoons vegetable oil
1 small onion, cut in ½-inch pieces
1 large shallot, minced
2 teaspoons minced fresh ginger
½ teaspoon curry powder
¼ teaspoon ground coriander
⅛ to ¼ teaspoon cayenne
1 large eggplant, peeled and cut in
  1-inch cubes

⅔ cup Chicken Stock (page 25) or
  canned broth, or Vegetable Stock
  (page 24)
1 tablespoon seasoned rice vinegar
¼ cup chopped fresh cilantro or
  parsley
Salt

---

1. Heat the oil in the pressure cooker over medium-high heat. Add the onion, shallot, ginger, curry powder, coriander, and cayenne. Cook uncovered, stirring often, until onion begins to soften, about 3 minutes. Add the eggplant, stock or broth, and vinegar.

2. Cover and place over high heat. Start timing immediately and cook 3 minutes. Release pressure and stir in the cilantro and salt to taste.

Braised Fennel with Lemon and Pepper

Fresh bulb fennel has a subtle, elegant taste, similar to celery but with a refined hint of anise. This preparation mimics a classic use of fennel, partnering it with lemon, pepper, and Parmesan cheese.

Makes 4 servings

---

3 tablespoons olive oil
1 large garlic clove, sliced
1 small dried red pepper
2 large fennel bulbs, trimmed, quartered lengthwise
¾ cup Chicken Stock (page 25) or canned broth, or Vegetable Stock (page 24)

¼ cup dry white wine
½ lemon
Salt and coarsely ground pepper
¼ cup freshly grated Parmesan cheese

---

1. Heat the oil, garlic, and dried pepper in the pressure cooker over medium-high heat. As soon as the garlic begins to color, remove it with a slotted spoon and discard it. Add the fennel, cut sides down, and cook uncovered, turning once, until lightly browned, about 8 minutes. Add stock or broth and wine.

2. Cover and bring up to high pressure. Reduce heat to stabilize pressure and cook 4 minutes. Release pressure by running cold water over lid.

3. To serve, remove the fennel from cooking liquid. Squeeze the lemon juice over the fennel and season with salt and pepper to taste. Sprinkle the cheese on top.

City Slicker Greens

Many an old-time cook thinks greens are strictly within the realm of the country cousins. There's folly in that logic, and here's an updated and thoroughly delightful way to shrug off any outmoded notions about greens.

Makes 3 to 4 servings

---

1 large bunch of collard greens
1 tablespoon unsalted butter
1 small onion, chopped
1 small red bell pepper, finely diced
1 teaspoon sugar
½ cup Chicken Stock (page 25) or
    canned broth, or Vegetable Stock
    (page 24)

½ teaspoon salt
Dash of cayenne
1½ teaspoons red wine vinegar

---

1. Rinse collards well. Trim away thick center rib and cut leaves into 1½-inch squares.
2. Melt the butter in the pressure cooker. Add the onion and bell pepper. Cook uncovered over medium heat until soft, 3 to 4 minutes. Add the sugar and cook until syrupy, 1 to 2 minutes. Add the collards, stock or broth, salt, and cayenne.
3. Cover and bring up to high pressure. Reduce heat to stabilize pressure and cook 5 minutes. Release pressure, stir in the vinegar, and serve.

Summer Green Beans with Tomato and Pesto

Makes 4 servings

1 pound green beans, trimmed
1 medium tomato, finely diced
3 to 4 tablespoons prepared pesto
   sauce

Salt and freshly ground pepper

1. Place the beans in pressure cooker with 1 cup water. Place over high heat with cover locked in place. Start timing immediately and cook for 4 minutes. Release pressure by running cold water over the cover.
2. Drain the beans and transfer to a serving dish. Toss with the tomato, pesto, and salt and pepper to taste. Serve hot or at room temperature.

Cajun Okra with Tomatoes

Okra has been unfairly shunned by many who malign it for being slimy. Lightly cooked, it shows no such tendencies.

Makes 4 to 6 servings

---

2 slices of bacon, diced
1 small onion, chopped
2 celery ribs, sliced
½ teaspoon dried thyme
¼ teaspoon celery seed

12 ounces okra, trimmed, cut crosswise
　　into thirds
1 can (14½ ounces) Cajun-style stewed
　　tomatoes
Salt and cayenne

---

1. Cook the bacon in the pressure cooker uncovered over medium heat until it begins to render some fat, about 2 minutes. Add the onion, celery, thyme, and celery seed and cook until bacon is crisp, 3 to 4 minutes longer. Add the okra and tomatoes with their liquid.

2. Cover and place over high heat. Start timing immediately and cook 4 minutes. Release pressure by running cold water over the lid. Season with salt and cayenne to taste.

Creamy Braised Potatoes and Leeks
with Bacon

When potatoes are cut into small cubes, they cook in the pressure cooker as quickly as leeks.

Makes 4 servings

---

2 strips of smoked bacon, diced
2 medium yellow or red potatoes
  (about 12 ounces), cut in ½-inch
  cubes
3 medium leeks (white and tender
  green), cut in 1½-inch lengths
½ cup Chicken Stock (page 25) or
  canned broth

1 teaspoon fresh thyme or ½ teaspoon
  dried thyme
3 tablespoons whipping cream
¼ teaspoon salt
⅛ teaspoon freshly ground pepper

---

1. Cook the bacon in the pressure cooker uncovered over medium heat until it is browned and the fat is rendered, about 5 minutes. Remove the bacon with a slotted spoon and set aside. Add the potatoes to the cooker and cook over medium heat for 2 minutes. Add the leeks, stock or broth, and thyme.

2. Cover and turn to high heat. Begin timing immediately and cook 4 minutes. Release pressure by running cold water over the lid. Add the cream, salt, and pepper. Boil over high heat uncovered 45 seconds to thicken slightly. Add the reserved bacon and serve.

Eccentric Mashed Potatoes

What's so eccentric about these luscious mashed potatoes? They're inspired by an Oprah Winfrey favorite that's served at Eccentric, a Chicago restaurant in which she's a partner. And besides, as mashed potatoes go, these lumpy potatoes, served with skin and all, are wonderfully offbeat.

Makes 8 servings

1½ pounds red potatoes, scrubbed and cut in chunks
1½ pounds Idaho potatoes, scrubbed and cut in chunks

1 small onion, quartered
3 tablespoons unsalted butter
½ cup horseradish sauce
Salt

---

1. Combine the red potatoes, Idaho potatoes, and onion in the pressure cooker. Add enough salted water to cover. Cover and bring up to high pressure. Reduce heat to stabilize pressure and cook 10 minutes. Release pressure.

2. Drain the potatoes; return to the cooker. Stir briefly over low heat to dry excess water. Mash with a potato masher. Add butter; when it melts, blend in the horseradish sauce. Season with salt to taste. Mix until light and fluffy.

Salsa Spuds

Gravy becomes extraneous with these sassy mashed potatoes. Use your favorite salsa, either freshly made or bottled. Smoked tomato salsa is an excellent choice.

Makes 6 servings

1½ pounds red potatoes, scrubbed and cut in 1½-inch pieces
3 carrots, peeled and sliced
1 medium onion, quartered

⅓ cup prepared tomato salsa
¾ cup shredded cheese, such as Chihuahua, Cheddar, or Monterey Jack
Salt and cayenne

---

1. Combine the potatoes, carrots, and onion in the pressure cooker. Add enough water to cover. Cover and bring up to high pressure. Reduce heat to stabilize pressure and cook 8 minutes. Release pressure.
2. Drain well and return the vegetables to the pressure cooker. Stir briefly over low heat to dry excess moisture. Mash with a potato masher. Blend in salsa and cheese. Season with salt and cayenne to taste.

Orange-Glazed Root Vegetables

Carrots and orange have a special affinity for each other. Here it is extended to parsnips, too. Rutabagas, sometimes called yellow turnips or Swedes, can be added as well.

Makes 3 to 4 servings

---

2 large carrots, peeled
2 medium parsnips, peeled
1 tablespoon unsalted butter
½ cup Chicken Stock (page 25) or
    canned broth
1 tablespoon orange marmalade, prefer-
    ably bitter orange

1 tablespoon cider vinegar
½ teaspoon grated orange zest
Dash of cayenne
⅛ teaspoon salt

---

1. Cut the carrots and parsnips crosswise into thirds. Cut each third lengthwise into quarters.

2. Melt the butter in the pressure cooker over high heat. Add the carrots and parsnips. Cook uncovered, stirring often, until they begin to soften and brown at the edges, 2 minutes. Add the stock or broth, marmalade, vinegar, orange zest, and cayenne.

3. Cover the pressure cooker. Start timing immediately and cook 4 minutes. Release pressure by running cold water over the cover. Add salt and boil uncovered until the liquid is thick and syrupy, 1½ to 2 minutes.

Red Curry Squash

Winter squash, all too often baked with butter and sugar, takes a decidedly spicy turn when it's prepared with a Thai touch. Butternut squash is recommended over acorn squash, since it's so much easier to peel when it's raw.

Makes 4 to 6 servings

1½ tablespoons vegetable oil
1 small onion, chopped
2 pounds butternut squash, peeled and
  cut in 1-inch chunks
½ cup Chicken Stock (page 25) or
  canned broth, or Vegetable Stock
  (page 24)

¼ cup coconut milk
1 to 2 teaspoons Thai red curry paste
Salt

---

1. Heat the oil in the pressure cooker over high heat. Add the onion and cook uncovered until it begins to brown at the edges, 4 to 5 minutes. Add the squash and cook 1 minute. Combine the stock or broth, coconut milk, and curry paste; add to pressure cooker.

2. Cover and place over high heat. Start timing immediately and cook 6 minutes. Release pressure by running cold water over the lid. Season with salt to taste.

Spaghetti Squash

There's a certain wonderful whimsy in cutting open a spaghetti squash and seeing from whence the name comes. The interior flesh separates into a mass of slender, pastalike strands that can be served plain or topped with sauces, stews, sautéed vegetables, or just a sprinkling of cheese. One option is offered here; many await.

Makes 4 servings

---

1 small spaghetti squash, 2 pounds
2 tablespoons olive oil
1 large garlic clove, minced

2 tablespoons minced fresh basil
½ teaspoon salt
Dash of crushed hot pepper flakes

---

1. Make a slash through the exterior skin of the squash, going from stem to stem and cutting about ½ inch deep. Put in pressure cooker with 2 cups of water. Cover and bring up to high pressure. Reduce heat to stabilize pressure and cook 20 minutes. Let pressure release naturally. Drain.

2. Cut the squash in half, roughly following the original slash in the skin. Scoop out and discard the seeds and spongy membrane from the center. Transfer the squash to a bowl and separate into strands, using 2 forks. Blend in the olive oil, garlic, basil, salt, and hot pepper flakes; serve hot.

Mashed Sweet Potatoes and Carrots

Loaded with vitamins, this vibrant vegetable puree is easy to prepare and reheats very well. Honey can replace the maple syrup, if desired.

Makes 4 to 6 servings

1¼ pounds sweet potatoes, peeled and cut into ½-inch slices

3 large carrots, peeled and cut into ½-inch slices

2 tablespoons unsalted butter

2 tablespoons sour cream

2 tablespoons maple syrup

1 tablespoon fresh lemon juice

½ teaspoon salt

¼ teaspoon grated nutmeg

⅛ teaspoon ground coriander

⅛ teaspoon freshly ground pepper

---

1. Combine the sweet potatoes and carrots in the pressure cooker and add 1 cup water. Cover and bring up to high pressure. Reduce heat to stabilize pressure and cook 8 minutes. Release pressure.

2. Drain off any excess water, place cooker over high heat, and toss vegetables briefly, uncovered, to dry out. Transfer to a blender or food processor and add all the remaining ingredients. Puree until smooth.

Indonesian Vegetable Medley

A unique pairing of vegetables and spices results in a colorful array of textures and tastes. Because all of these stalwart vegetables are available in winter, this dish has a remarkable ability to add a touch of summer to the harsher times of year.

Makes 6 servings

---

1 tablespoon vegetable oil
1 small onion, cut in thin wedges
1½ teaspoons minced fresh ginger
½ teaspoon ground cumin
½ teaspoon paprika
½ teaspoon salt
⅛ teaspoon cayenne
½ medium head of green cabbage, cut in ½-inch ribbons

3 large carrots, sliced
¼ pound green beans, cut in 1-inch pieces
½ cup unsweetened coconut milk
¼ cup Vegetable Stock (page 24), canned broth, or water
2 tablespoons chopped fresh mint
2 tablespoons chopped roasted peanuts

---

1. Heat the oil in the pressure cooker. Add the onion and cook uncovered over medium-high heat until it begins to soften, 3 to 4 minutes. Add the ginger, cumin, paprika, salt, and cayenne; cook 1 minute. Add the cabbage, carrots, green beans, coconut milk, and stock or broth.

2. Cover and place over high heat. Start timing immediately and cook 6 minutes. Release pressure by running cold water over the lid. Stir in the mint and sprinkle the peanuts over the top.

Summer Vegetable Stew

Stews often signal winter, but in this rendition the best of summer comes to mind. For even cooking, be sure to cut the vegetables as directed so the firmer ones cook and the tender varieties don't overcook.

Makes 4 to 6 servings

1 tablespoon olive oil
2 medium leeks (white part only), cut in ½-inch slices
1 medium eggplant, peeled and cut in 1-inch cubes
3 medium zucchini or yellow squash or a mix of both, cut in ¾-inch cubes

1 large red potato, cut in ½-inch cubes
1 red bell pepper, cut in ¾-inch cubes
1 cup meatless tomato pasta sauce
3 tablespoons prepared pesto sauce
Salt and freshly ground pepper

1. Heat the oil in the pressure cooker. Add the leeks, eggplant, zucchini, potato, bell pepper, and tomato sauce.

2. Cover and place over high heat. Start timing immediately and cook 6 minutes. Release pressure by running cold water over the cover. Stir in the pesto sauce and season with salt and pepper to taste. Serve warm or at room temperature.

Winter Curry Vegetables

Vegetables come to the forefront in this exotically spiced meatless main course. The curry, a simple blend of only three spices, adds well-defined taste to the vegetables.

Makes 4 servings

2 tablespoons olive oil
1 large garlic clove, minced
1 jalapeño or serrano pepper, minced
¾ teaspoon ground cumin
⅛ teaspoon cinnamon
⅛ teaspoon ground turmeric
3 large carrots, sliced
3 celery ribs, sliced
2 medium red bell peppers, cut in ¾-inch squares
1 large sweet potato, cut in ⅜-inch dice

1 small onion, chopped
1 can (16 ounces) garbanzo beans, drained
¼ cup dried currants
¾ cup Vegetable Stock (page 24), Chicken Stock (page 25), or canned broth
¼ cup orange juice
Salt and cayenne

1. Heat the oil in the pressure cooker over medium heat. Add the garlic, jalapeño pepper, cumin, cinnamon, and turmeric. Cook uncovered, stirring often, until the garlic begins to soften, 4 to 5 minutes. Add the carrots, celery, bell peppers, sweet potato, and onion and cook 1 minute. Add the garbanzo beans, currants, stock or broth, and orange juice.

2. Cover and bring up to high pressure. Reduce heat to stabilize pressure and cook 4 minutes. Release pressure. Add salt and cayenne to taste.

Caponata

Sweet and pungent, this thick, chunky Italian relish can be used atop salads and grilled fish or chicken, folded into frittatas, or tossed into pasta salads.

Makes 3 cups

2½ tablespoons olive oil

1 pound eggplant, preferably Italian or Japanese, unpeeled and cut in 1-inch cubes

1 medium onion, chopped

2 small celery ribs, sliced ½ inch thick

1 medium zucchini, quartered lengthwise, sliced ½ inch thick

½ cup tomato sauce

¼ cup red wine vinegar

¼ cup water

2 tablespoons tomato paste

2 tablespoons dried currants

1½ tablespoons drained capers

1 tablespoon sugar

3 tablespoons minced parsley

Salt

---

1. Heat the oil in the pressure cooker over medium heat. Add the eggplant and cook, stirring often, until it begins to brown, about 3 minutes. Add the onion, celery, and zucchini; cook 30 seconds. Add the tomato sauce, vinegar, water, tomato paste, currants, capers, and sugar.

2. Cover and bring up to high pressure. Turn off heat as soon as high pressure is reached. Leave cover locked and let stand at least 30 minutes. Uncover, stir in the parsley, and season with salt to taste. Serve chilled or at room temperature.

Desserts

Desserts in the pressure cooker? Absolutely! They are a sweet success—the crowning finish to a full range of recipes that pressure handles so well. Though there are limits to what types of desserts can be made in the pressure cooker (no cakes, pies, or cookies), there is a delicious handful of sweets that cook extraordinarily well there.

In seeming defiance of all that we know about egg cookery, custard desserts emerge from the pressure cooker with the most sublime texture imaginable. I've never had better results with flan and no longer consider baking them. Cheesecakes turn out airy and light, though they still have the creamy, rich texture that is their hallmark. Bread puddings and rice puddings are sensational. And simple fruit preparations, healthy, low-fat but fabulous alternatives, are perfect candidates for pressure cooking.

Hints and tips:
- Before you begin making a recipe, make sure you have an appropriate baking dish. It must fit easily into the cooker, with at least an inch of space between the dish and the sides of the pressure cooker. Also, it must rest on the steamer insert in a stable, level position. There's a good chance your collection already includes several dishes that are suitable.

- All baking dishes must be wrapped carefully so they are 100 percent sealed. You want to avoid any chance of water seeping inside.
- For easy removal of baking dishes, make a foil strip lift-handle. Tear a length of aluminum foil—I prefer heavy-duty foil—that will completely surround the sides and bottom of the casserole and extend beyond it by about one foot. Fold it in half lengthwise, then in half again so you end up with a very long strip. Place the baking dish on it and fold the ends over to make a handle. You can save the handle for other uses.
- Custards and cheesecakes must be lifted off the bottom of the cooker with a trivet. If your pressure cooker doesn't have a trivet, one can be fashioned from a small, heatproof plate.

Spiced Compote of Fresh Fruit

A haunting mix of spices and a light sugar syrup, supported by dried cherries, embrace just about any combination of fruit throughout the seasons. In winter, pears, apple, bananas, grapes, and pineapple make a fine medley. Summertime offers seemingly endless possibilities, among them berries, peaches, apricots, nectarines, plums, and cherries.

Makes 6 servings

---

1 cup water
⅓ cup orange juice
⅓ cup sugar
¼ cup dried tart cherries or dried cranberries
Juice and zest of 1 lemon

4 whole allspice berries
4 whole cloves
2 green cardamom pods, if available
5 cups mixed fresh fruit, cut in bite-size pieces
Fresh mint sprigs, for garnish

---

1. Combine all the ingredients except the fresh fruit and mint in the pressure cooker. Cover and bring up to high pressure. Release pressure.

2. Add firm fruits, such as pears and apples, when syrup still is very hot. Add softer fruits as the syrup cools but is still warm. Let stand at least 2 hours before serving. Fruits in syrup can be refrigerated overnight. Garnish each serving with fresh mint, if desired.

Wine-Mulled Peaches

Mulling spices and red wine infuse peaches with warmth and aroma. The peaches are left unpeeled for poaching; this magically transfers the reddish blush from the skin onto the peach. Then, so they are best able to soak up flavors, they are peeled shortly after cooking.

Makes 6 servings

1¾ cups fruity red wine, such as
   Beaujolais
¾ cup sugar
¼ cup water
3 cardamom pods
1 cinnamon stick

3 whole allspice berries
1 strip of orange zest, about 3 inches
   long
1 strip of lemon zest, about 2 inches
   long
6 large firm peaches

---

1. Combine the wine, sugar, and water in the pressure cooker. Scrape the seeds from cardamom into the mixture and add the cinnamon stick, allspice, orange zest, and lemon zest. Heat to a boil. Carefully add the peaches.

2. Cover and bring up to high pressure. Reduce heat to stabilize pressure and cook 2 minutes. Let pressure release naturally.

3. Carefully slip the skins from the peaches and return them to the hot poaching liquid. Refrigerate until well chilled. Serve peaches plain in syrup or over ice cream. Or the poaching liquid can be boiled until it is thick and syrupy and spooned over the peaches.

Honey-Lemon Pear Compote

The herbal minty taste of rosemary adds a hard-to-pin-down but distinctively delicious taste to pears. A handful of pomegranate seeds added to the syrup at serving time is a pretty addition.

Makes 4 servings

---

3 tablespoons honey
3 tablespoons sugar
1 sprig of rosemary
Juice of 1 lemon

½ cup dry white wine
¼ cup water
4 large firm but ripe pears, peeled,
    cored, and cut in 8 wedges each

---

1. Combine the honey and sugar in the pressure cooker. Cook uncovered over high heat, stirring often, until the mixture is smooth and bubbly, 3 to 4 minutes. Add the rosemary and lemon juice and cook 1 minute. Add the wine, water, and pears.
2. Cover and bring up to high pressure. Remove from heat as soon as high pressure is reached. Release pressure by running cold water over the cover. Remove pears with a slotted spoon.
3. Boil the liquid uncovered until it is slightly thickened, 2 to 3 minutes. Let it cool to lukewarm, then pour it over the pears and refrigerate until well chilled. Remove the rosemary at serving time.

Red Rosy Applesauce

A handful of cranberries adds an underlying tart tang and a delicate pink glow. The perfect time to make this is when cranberries just come into the market and autumn apples still are plentiful

Makes 3 cups

2½ pounds cooking apples, preferably
    a mix of varieties, peeled, cored,
    and quartered
½ cup cranberries
¼ cup apple cider

¼ cup maple syrup
¼ cup orange-flavored liqueur, such as
    Cointreau
1 tablespoon light brown sugar
1 cinnamon stick

---

1. Combine all the ingredients in the pressure cooker. Cover and bring up to high pressure. Cook 1 minute. Release pressure naturally.

2. Remove the cinnamon stick and puree the apple mixture in a food processor or blender. Serve warm or chilled.

Bourbon and Vanilla Pears

Light and delicate, these pears are kissed with the heady taste and aroma of vanilla and bourbon. At brunch, they can be served plain or as a topping for waffles. More traditionally, they make a fine dessert, either with ice cream or frozen yogurt, or plain.

Makes 4 to 6 servings

¾ cup sugar
2¾ cups water
1 cinnamon stick
2 whole cloves
1 strip of lemon zest, about 3 inches long, removed with a vegetable peeler

4 firm but ripe Comice pears, peeled, cored, and quartered lengthwise
2½ tablespoons bourbon
1 tablespoon vanilla extract
Juice of ½ lemon

1. Combine the sugar, ¼ cup of the water, the cinnamon stick, and cloves in the pressure cooker, stirring so the sugar is uniformly moistened. Cook uncovered over high heat until the syrup turns a medium tan color, 5 to 6 minutes. Carefully add remaining 2½ cups water; the caramel will harden. Cook until it melts again, 2 minutes. Add the lemon zest and pears.

2. Cover and bring up to high pressure. Reduce heat to stabilize pressure and cook 2 minutes. Release pressure by running cold water over the lid. Add the bourbon, vanilla, and lemon juice. Let pears cool in syrup. Refrigerate for up to 3 days.

Burnt Caramel Coffee Custard

It defies logic that the superheated pressure cooker could produce the most delicate and sublimely light custards, but it does just that. This one, the color of café au lait, is supremely rich, with an intense caramel flavor.

Makes 8 servings

1 tablespoon instant espresso powder	2½ cups whipping cream
¼ cup hot water	2 large eggs
1 cup sugar	4 large egg yolks

1. Dissolve the espresso powder in hot water; set aside. Put the sugar in a large heavy saucepan. Cook over high heat until sugar melts and turns a rich caramel color. As it cooks, swirl the pan so the sugar melts evenly. Add the espresso mixture and cream. Carefully stir with a long-handled spoon; the mixture will let off poufs of steam and the sugar will harden into a crystallized mass. Cook until the sugar melts again and the mixture is smooth. Remove from heat and let cool to lukewarm.
2. Whisk the eggs and egg yolks until smooth. Slowly whisk them into the cooled espresso cream, mixing thoroughly. Strain into a 7- to 8-cup casserole that will fit easily into the pressure cooker. Cover the casserole tightly with aluminum foil so no water can get inside.
3. Put a trivet in the pressure cooker and add 2 cups water. Carefully add the casserole. Cover and bring up to high pressure. Reduce heat to stabilize pressure and cook 20 minutes. Release pressure naturally. Remove casserole and carefully lift off foil. Let custard cool, then refrigerate at least 4 hours before serving.

Eggnog Flan

Eggnog is one of the wonderful rich excesses of the holiday season. Appropriately enough, it is sublime in a custard flan. For a classic all-seasons version, use a cup of whole milk in place of the eggnog.

Makes 8 to 10 servings

½ cup sugar

¼ teaspoon freshly grated nutmeg

2 large eggs

6 large egg yolks

1 can (14 ounces) sweetened condensed milk

1 can (12 ounces) evaporated whole milk

1 cup dairy eggnog

1 teaspoon dark rum

1 teaspoon brandy

1 teaspoon vanilla extract

---

1. Put the sugar and ⅛ teaspoon of the nutmeg in a small heavy saucepan. Cook over medium-high heat, watching closely, until the sugar melts and takes on a rich amber color. Immediately pour into a 6½-cup ring mold that fits easily inside the pressure cooker. Cushioning your hand with a mitt, tilt the mold so the caramel covers the bottom and sides.

2. In a large mixing bowl, whisk the eggs and egg yolks until well combined. Blend in the condensed milk, evaporated milk, eggnog, rum, brandy, and remaining ⅛ teaspoon nutmeg. Mix well, then strain through a fine strainer. Pour the custard into the caramel-coated mold. Wrap the mold in foil so no water can get inside.

3. Put a trivet in the pressure cooker and add 2 cups water. Carefully place the mold on the trivet. Cover the pressure cooker and bring up to high pressure. Reduce heat to stabilize pressure and cook 20 minutes. Release pressure naturally. Carefully remove the mold and lift off the foil. Let the flan cool to room temperature, then refrigerate at least 4 hours before serving. To serve, carefully loosen the flan from the sides of the mold with a small knife. Hold a serving plate on top and quickly invert to unmold.

Tropical Coconut Lime Flan

Seductively rich and smooth, this caramel-topped flan surprises with cool tropical flavors.

Makes 8 to 10 servings

¾ cup sugar

3 large eggs

4 large egg yolks

1 can (14 ounces) sweetened condensed milk

1 cup unsweetened coconut milk

1 cup whole milk

2 tablespoons finely minced fresh ginger

1 teaspoon finely minced lime zest

2 teaspoons light rum

---

1. Put ½ cup of the sugar in a small heavy saucepan. Cook over medium-high heat, watching closely, until the sugar melts and turns a rich amber brown. Immediately pour into a 6½-cup ring mold that fits easily into the pressure cooker. Cushioning your hand with a mitt, tilt the mold so the caramel covers the bottom and sides.

2. In a large bowl, whisk the remaining ¼ cup sugar into the eggs and egg yolks. Add the condensed milk, coconut milk, and whole milk; mix well. Strain through a fine strainer. Put the minced ginger in a piece of cheesecloth or a single ply of paper toweling. Working over the flan mixture, squeeze firmly to extract as much juice as possible from the ginger. Add the lime zest and rum and mix well.

3. Pour the custard into the caramel-coated mold. Cover tightly with aluminum foil so no water can get inside. Place a trivet in the pressure cooker and add 2 cups water. Carefully add the mold. Cover the pressure cooker and bring up to high pressure. Reduce heat to stabilize pressure and cook 20 minutes. Release pressure. Carefully remove mold and foil. Let cool to room temperature, then refrigerate at least 4 hours before serving. To serve, carefully loosen the flan from the sides of the mold. Hold a serving plate on top and quickly invert to unmold.

Desserts

Gingered Rice Pudding

Makes 6 servings

½ cup medium- or short-grain white
   rice
1½ cups milk
½ cup water
1 large egg
2 large egg yolks

½ cup sugar
Freshly grated nutmeg
1 cup whipping cream
2 tablespoons finely minced crystallized
   ginger
1 teaspoon vanilla extract

---

1. Combine the rice, ½ cup of the milk, and the water in a pressure cooker. Cover and bring up to high pressure. Reduce heat to stabilize pressure and cook 6 minutes. Release pressure by running cold water over cover. Let stand, covered, 5 minutes.

2. In a medium bowl, whisk together the egg, egg yolks, sugar, and nutmeg. Blend in the remaining 1 cup milk and the cream, mixing well. Stir in the crystallized ginger and vanilla. Fold in the cooked rice. Transfer to a buttered 6- to 7-cup casserole that fits easily inside the pressure cooker. Cover the casserole tightly with aluminum foil so no water can get inside.

3. Put a trivet in the pressure cooker and add 2 cups water. Add the casserole. Cover the pressure cooker and bring up to high pressure. Reduce heat to stabilize pressure and cook 12 minutes. Release pressure; remove foil and stir mixture. Cover tightly again. Return to high pressure and cook 10 minutes. Let pressure release naturally. Serve warm or chilled.

Chocolate Orange Pots de Crème

In truth, this fancy name and sensuously rich dessert is closely akin to chocolate pudding. Though most commonly served chilled, it is good warm, too—for those who can't wait.

Makes 4 servings

¾ cup whole milk
½ cup half-and-half or light cream
Zest of 1 tangerine, removed in long strands with a vegetable peeler
3 ounces semisweet chocolate, finely chopped

¼ cup sugar
4 large egg yolks, lightly beaten
2 teaspoons orange-flavored liqueur, such as Grand Marnier
Whipped cream, as accompaniment

---

1. Combine the milk, half-and-half, and tangerine zest in a medium saucepan. Heat to a simmer and let stand, covered, for 10 minutes. Remove and discard the zest. Add the chocolate and sugar to the warm liquid; let stand, uncovered, 5 minutes. Whisk until smooth. Add the egg yolks and liqueur and mix well.

2. Divide custard among four ⅔-cup ramekins. Cover them tightly with aluminum foil so no water can get inside. Put a trivet in the pressure cooker and add 1½ cups water. Arrange the ramekins on the trivet.

3. Cover and bring up to high pressure. Reduce heat to stabilize pressure and cook 12 minutes. Release pressure naturally. Carefully remove the ramekins and foil; let cool 20 minutes. Serve warm with whipped cream, if desired. Or cover lightly and refrigerate at least 3 hours or overnight before serving.

Chocolate Caramel Custard

Dark and rich with chocolate, this custard is divine in its own right. Served atop a thin layer of cake, it's sublime. Pound cake or sponge cake can be used, and either one can be store-bought rather than homemade.

Makes 6 servings

½ cup plus 2 tablespoons sugar

3 ounces semisweet chocolate, finely chopped

2 cups whipping cream, scalded

5 large egg yolks, lightly beaten

1 teaspoon vanilla extract

2 slices, each about ½ inch thick, pound cake or sponge cake

---

1. Put ½ cup of the sugar in a small heavy saucepan. Cook over medium-high heat until the sugar melts and takes on a rich caramel color. Immediately pour into a 4- to 6-cup round baking dish that easily fits inside your pressure cooker. Cushioning your hand with a pot holder, tilt the pan so caramel covers bottom in a smooth, even layer, set aside.

2. Put the chocolate and remaining 2 tablespoons sugar in a medium bowl; add hot cream. Let stand 10 minutes, then whisk until smooth. Whisk in egg yolks and vanilla, blending well. Pour into caramel-lined baking dish. Cover tightly with aluminum foil, making sure no water can get inside.

3. Put a trivet in the pressure cooker and add 2 cups water. Set the baking dish on the trivet. Cover and bring up to high pressure. Reduce heat to stabilize pressure and cook 23 minutes. Release pressure naturally.

4. Carefully remove the dish and uncover. Let cool, cover, and refrigerate at least 4 hours before serving. To serve, loosen the custard from the sides of the dish with a small knife. Trim the cake slices as necessary and arrange on top of the custard. (It's okay if the cake is pieced.) Hold a large serving plate over the baking dish and quickly invert.

Brown Sugar Bread Pudding

Makes 6 to 8 servings

4 tablespoons unsalted butter, softened	½ cup granulated sugar
8 slices of oatmeal bread	⅓ cup light brown sugar
2 large eggs	2 teaspoons vanilla extract
2 large egg yolks	2 cups half-and-half or light cream

1. Use 1 tablespoon of the butter to grease a 7- to 8-cup casserole that fits easily inside the pressure cooker. Use the rest to butter the bread. Stack the bread and cut into 1-inch squares.

2. In a medium bowl, whisk together the eggs, egg yolks, granulated sugar, brown sugar, and vanilla. Blend in the cream, mixing well. Add the bread cubes and let stand 15 minutes, until the bread is soaked. Transfer to the casserole and cover tightly with aluminum foil so no water can get inside.

3. Put a trivet in the pressure cooker and add 3 cups water. Carefully place the casserole on the trivet. Cover and bring up to high pressure. Reduce heat to stabilize pressure and cook 20 minutes. Release pressure naturally. Serve warm or chilled.

Banana Bread Pudding

A comforting concoction with flavors that take a look back to childhood. It can be served plain, but many find the temptation to add hot fudge sauce too hard to resist.

Makes 6 to 8 servings

---

4 tablespoons unsalted butter

8 slices of cinnamon raisin bread

2 small ripe bananas, sliced about ½ inch thick

2 large eggs

2 large egg yolks

1 cup sugar

1¾ cups half-and-half or light cream

1½ teaspoons vanilla extract

1½ teaspoons dark rum

---

1. Use 1 tablespoon of the butter to grease a 7- to 8-cup casserole that fits easily into the pressure cooker. Use the rest to butter the bread. Stack the bread and cut the slices into quarters.

2. Spread about one quarter of the bread in the bottom of the buttered casserole. Top with about one third of the bananas. Continue layering bread and bananas, ending with a layer of bread. Whisk together the eggs, egg yolks, and sugar until light. Blend in the cream, vanilla, and rum, mixing well. Pour the custard over the bread. Press the top slices of bread down so they are well soaked with the custard.

3. Cover the casserole with foil so no water can get inside. Place a trivet in the pressure cooker and add 2 cups water. Set the casserole on the trivet. Cover and bring up to high pressure. Reduce heat to stabilize pressure and cook 22 minutes. Release pressure naturally. Chill the pudding thoroughly before serving.

Native Maple Spice Pudding

Sometimes called Indian pudding, this is a variant of one of the first desserts colonists put together with the foods native to their new land. It is more of a soft, sweet cereal than a pudding and is thoroughly delightful to those who take pleasure in simple desserts.

Makes 6 servings

2¼ cups whole milk
¾ cup whipping cream
6 tablespoons fine cornmeal
½ teaspoon cinnamon
½ teaspoon allspice
¼ teaspoon freshly grated nutmeg

⅛ teaspoon salt
½ cup maple syrup
3 tablespoons brown sugar
2 tablespoons unsalted butter
1 teaspoon vanilla extract

---

1. Heat milk and cream uncovered in the pressure cooker to just below the boil. Very slowly whisk in cornmeal (if it is added too quickly, lumps will form). Stir in the cinnamon, allspice, nutmeg, and salt. Cook over medium heat, stirring occasionally, until the mixture comes to a boil. Remove from the heat and blend in the maple syrup, brown sugar, butter, and vanilla. Transfer to a 6- to 7-cup casserole that fits easily inside the pressure cooker. Cover tightly with aluminum foil so no water can get inside. Rinse out the pressure cooker.

2. Put a trivet inside the pressure cooker and add 2 cups water. Set the casserole on the trivet. Cover and bring up to high pressure. Reduce heat to stabilize pressure and cook 30 minutes. Release pressure naturally. Serve the pudding warm.

Classic Cheesecake

This is indisputably one of the favorite desserts of all time. If you prefer an Italian ricotta cheesecake, use only two packages of cream cheese along with one cup of ricotta cheese.

Makes 8 servings

1½ pounds (three 8-ounce packages) cream cheese, softened
1 cup plus 2 tablespoons sugar
3 large eggs

¼ cup whipping cream
2 tablespoons all-purpose flour
3 teaspoons vanilla extract
1 cup sour cream

---

1. In a large bowl, beat the cream cheese and 1 cup of the sugar with an electric mixer on high speed for 3 minutes. Add the eggs, one at a time, mixing well after each addition. Continue beating 2 minutes. Add the cream, flour, and 2 teaspoons of the vanilla; mix well.

2. Transfer the batter to a lightly buttered 7-inch springform pan. Wrap tightly in aluminum foil so no water can get inside. Put a trivet in the pressure cooker and add 3 cups water. Carefully put the pan on the trivet.

3. Cover and bring up to high pressure. Reduce heat to stabilize pressure and cook 40 minutes. Release pressure naturally. Carefully remove foil. The cake should be barely set in the center. Cool to room temperature.

4. To make a topping, combine the sour cream with the remaining 2 tablespoons sugar and 1 teaspoon vanilla; mix until smooth. Spread over the top of the cheesecake. Cover and refrigerate at least 4 hours before serving.

Fuzzy Navel Cheesecake

Those who know and love the refreshing summer drink known as a "fuzzy navel" need no further explanation or urging to try this creamy concoction that bears its name. For those who are as yet unaware, a fuzzy navel is made from orange juice, peach schnapps, and a dose of vodka. These flavors, sans vodka, do wondrous things for cheesecake. The peach topping described below makes the prettiest presentation. When peaches aren't in season, a simple sour cream topping can be substituted.

Makes 8 servings

1½ pounds (three 8-ounce packages) cream cheese, softened

1¼ cups sugar

3 large eggs

¼ cup plus 1 tablespoon peach schnapps

3 tablespoons orange juice concentrate, undiluted

2 tablespoons all-purpose flour

2 large ripe peaches, halved lengthwise, pitted, and thinly sliced

2 teaspoons fresh lemon juice

¼ cup peach or apricot preserves, melted and strained

---

1. In a large bowl, beat the cream cheese and sugar with an electric mixer on high speed for 3 minutes. Add the eggs, one at a time, mixing well after each addition. Add ¼ cup of the schnapps, the orange juice concentrate, and the flour. Continue to beat for 2 minutes.

---

2. Transfer the batter to a lightly buttered 7-inch springform pan. Wrap tightly in aluminum foil so no water can get inside. Put a trivet in the pressure cooker and add 3 cups water. Carefully set the pan on the trivet.

3. Cover and bring up to high pressure. Reduce heat to stabilize pressure and cook 40 minutes. Release pressure naturally. Carefully remove foil. Cake should be barely set in the center. Cool to room temperature.

4. For topping, toss peaches with lemon juice so they don't discolor. Arrange over top of cake in a radial design. Stir together preserves and remaining 1 tablespoon schnapps. Carefully brush over peaches and edge of cake. Refrigerate at least 3 hours before serving.

Index

Tomato(es) (*cont.*)
  green beans with pesto and, summer, 157
  okra with, Cajun, 158
  relish, pork chops with, 44
  sauce
    Basque, swordfish with, 65
    marinara, spicy, 100
    minted, Sicilian swordfish with, 63
    mushroom and, pasta, 102
    puttanesca, 103
    and sausage and sweet pepper, 101
  Tortellini with prosciutto and peas, 106
Tortilla vegetable soup, 14
Tropical coconut-lime flan, 180
Tuna
  steaks with sweet/sour onion relish, 64
  and white bean salad, 116
Turkey
  cabbage rolls stuffed with, 38
  chili, last-minute, 76
  in gumbo z'herbes, 70
Turnips, mashed celery root with apples
    and, 152
Tuscan pasta, potato, and bean soup, 17

V

Vanilla and bourbon pears, 176
Veal
  ragu, 98
  shanks Milanese, 48
  steaks with mixed pepper compote, 50
  stew with tangerine and cumin, 94
Vegetable(s), 142–43. *See also specific
    vegetables*
  and barley pilaf, 141
  curried, winter, 168

and fish, Chinese steamed, 53
  medley, Indonesian, 166
  pot roast with farm, 43
  risotto stew with beef and, 82
  root, oxtail stew with, 86
  soup, tortilla, 14
  stew
    beef and, 85
    summer, 167
  stock, 24
Vinegar, balsamic, honey-glazed carrots
    with, 151

W

Wehani Mexicani, 136
Wheat berry
  and basmati rice medley, 130
  tabbouleh, 139
White bean(s)
  with escarole, 115
  lamb shanks with, Provençal, 47
  and pasta and potato soup, Tuscan, 17
  stew with tomatoes, spinach, and mush-
    rooms, 118
  and tuna salad, 116
Whitefish en papillote, 60
Wild mushroom risotto, 135
Wild rice with pecans and dried cranberries,
    140
Wine-mulled peaches, 173
Winter curry vegetables, 168
Winter squash curry, red, 163

Z

Zucchini, summer corn with tomatoes and,
    153